6.00

Mindanao Mission

MINDANAO MISSION

Archbishop Patrick Cronin's Forty Years in the Philippines

EDWARD FISCHER

✠ ✠ ✠

A Crossroad Book | The Seabury Press | *New York*

1978 | *The Seabury Press*
815 Second Avenue | New York, N.Y. 10017

Library of Congress Cataloging in Publication Data

Fischer, Edward.   Mindanao mission
"A Crossroad book"
1. Cronin, Patrick, 1913– 2. Catholic Church—
Bishops—Biography. 3. Bishops—Philippine Islands—
Biography I. Title.
BX4705.C7834F57   266'.009599'7   78–12802
ISBN 0–8164–0412–7

To the benefactors
who made possible
Patrick Cronin's work
in the Philippines,
this book is dedicated.

Contents

Mindanao Mission

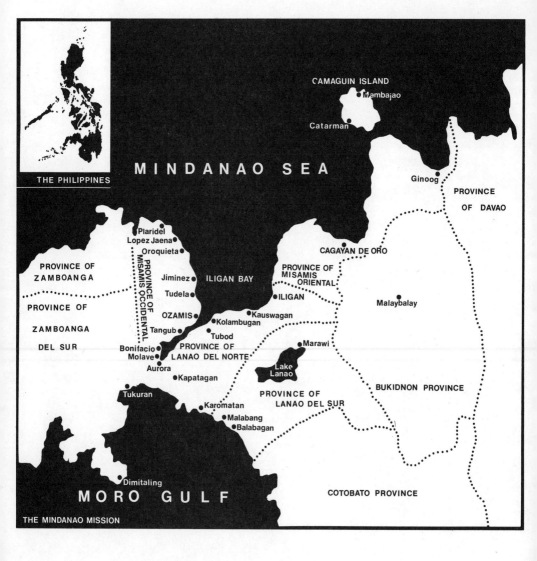

CAMAGUIN ISLAND
• Mambajao
Catarman •

MINDANAO SEA

Ginoog •

PROVINCE
OF DAVAO

PROVINCE OF
ZAMBOANGA

Plaridel •
Lopez Jaena •
Oroquieta •

PROVINCE OF MISAMIS OCCIDENTAL

Jiminez •

ILIGAN BAY

CAGAYAN DE ORO •

PROVINCE OF
MISAMIS
ORIENTAL

PROVINCE OF
ZAMBOANGA

Tudela •

DEL SUR

OZAMIS •
Tangub •

Kolambugan •
Tubod •

Kauswagan •
• ILIGAN

Malaybalay •

Bonifacio •
Molave •
Aurora •

PROVINCE OF
LANAO DEL NORTE

Marawi •

Lake
Lanao

• Kapatagan

PROVINCE OF
LANAO DEL SUR

BUKIDNON PROVINCE

Tukuran •

Karomatan •
• Malabang
• Balabagan

Dimitaling •

MORO GULF

COTOBATO PROVINCE

THE PHILIPPINES

THE MINDANAO MISSION

1 ✣ Murder in Mindanao

T wo sullen Moro students, one with a pistol and the other with
   a carbine, stalked across the school playground to within ten
feet of a young priest dressed in a white soutane. The priest, about
to climb into a jeep, paused and said, "Let's go into my office and
talk about it." Without a word they riddled him and he died
instantly.

When Bishop Patrick Cronin heard the news his mind would
scarcely accept it. Martin Dempsey dead! Murdered! He was always so humorous, so willing. Of the 260 Columbans in the Philippines none seemed more alive. Despite his thirty-six years Father
Dempsey had kept the lean, fresh look of a college boy right up
to that Monday morning.

When the bad news came, the bishop was getting ready to move
from Ozamis to Cagayan de Oro where he would become the new
archbishop. Now he put everything aside to hurry to Balabagan,
an isolated coastal town in Mindanao, accessible from the west by
sea, from the north by unreliable road, and from the air by light
plane. On the way down by road the bishop recalled with regret
that only within the month he had appointed Father Dempsey as
principal of the school at Balabagan, with its 350 students, mostly
Muslims. For most of his six years in the Philippines the young
priest had been an assistant pastor in the area.

In Balabagan the bishop found throngs of parishioners milling
around a house at the edge of the airstrip, a guest house owned
by the Lobregat coconut plantation, a temporary home for Father
Dempsey until his *convento* could be built. Wreaths of flowers
crowded the verandah and carried on into the hall where, leaning
against the stairway, was a simple white wooden cross inscribed
with the name of the deceased and the date of death, October 19,
1970. The body was laid out in an upstairs room.

Bishop Cronin soon learned in some detail of the events that led
to the tragedy: On Monday morning Father Dempsey had gone

to the school to attend the flag ceremony. He verbally corrected a fourteen-year-old student for an infringement of the rules. The boy got angry and reported the incident to his seventeen-year-old brother. The two of them confronted the priest, threatening to kill him. They departed and a short time later returned well armed.

The night before the funeral, the mayor of Balabagan and the bishop met to talk about the tragedy. The students on the playground had said that the mayor's sons killed Father Dempsey, but the mayor denied it.

On Thursday morning the procession left the guest house, moved down the airstrip and turned right along a half mile of dusty road to the village, which was nearly hidden among banana plants and coconut trees. All the way, in a blazing sun, the crowd recited the rosary while men took turns carrying the heavy coffin, making sure it never touched the ground.

The bishop, twenty-four Columbans, and two Filipino priests concelebrated the Requiem Mass in the simple open chapel with a galvanized roof. In the Visayan dialect the bishop spoke of Martin Dempsey, of love and forgiveness and peace. He mentioned that Martin was an only son, a remark that caused an outburst of uncontrolled weeping.

The only bright spot that Archbishop Cronin remembers from that day is that two priests approached him to offer themselves as replacements in Balabagan. Such a courageous commitment lifted his spirit. He knew the priests realized all too well that they were offering to spend their lives in Moro country. The archbishop appointed Father Burke, a scholarly man with a capacity for loneliness.

Father Dempsey's murder, like other dramatic events in Mindanao, caused Patrick Cronin to reflect on the unpredictable turns his life had taken. So often he is aware that between Moneygall and Mindanao lies a whole wide world. Moneygall, where he was born, is in the parish of Dunkerrin, the county of Offaly, the Diocese of Killaloe, in south central Ireland. Mindanao, not far above the equator, is the largest southern island in the Philippine archipelago.

In appearance the places are also a world apart. Moneygall and Tullamore, where he grew up, rest in a gentle valley between the

Sieve Bloom Mountains, a dairy country with rolling hills and twisting lanes held close by hedges and stone walls. The land bears little resemblance to Mindanao's spiny mountains, dense in jungle, with rivers dark and sluggish, crowded to the edges by tropical growth.

Culturally, the resemblance was also slight. The ways of doing things were different enough to cause Patrick Cronin to ask himself, Why me? Why should I have been chosen to help bridge the gap between East and West? The question has come up often in the forty years since he arrived in Mindanao as a newly ordained twenty-five-year-old. And yet Mindanao has always seemed the place where he was meant to be.

The differences have also puzzled and appalled Rosanna Fleming. Now in her eighties, she still lives across the street from the church where she held Patrick above the black stone baptismal font on the very day of his birth, November 30, 1913. The ceremony was held so hurriedly not because the child was sickly but because the priest would not return for a week or more.

Because her godson had become a missionary and had sailed for the Philippines, she followed closely every scrap of news about the Columbans and about Mindanao. Since the Columbans were founded in Ireland, the Irish press reported each time one of them died a violent death—nineteen in all: two in China, one in Burma, seven in Korea, one in Europe, and eight in the Philippines. Through the years, sixty-seven were arrested and held in internment or imprisoned.

In the news from Mindanao, Rosanna Fleming also heard about earthquakes, tidal waves, ambushes by Moros, American guerrilla fighters, and Japanese attacks. All of which helped her to conclude that Mindanao is not for the fainthearted.

2 ✢ School Days in Ireland

When Patrick was three years old, Sergeant Henry Cronin of the Royal Irish Constabulary, moved his family from Moneygall to Tullamore. It was during the time of The Troubles, or as the old Irish call it, "the war among brothers." Rosanna Fleming sighed, " 'Twas a sad time. 'Twas a bad time." The old pastor of Dunkerrin, Father Crosgrove, said, "The spirit of revenge was abroad in the land."

The Cronins felt the sad times with a special severity, especially on Halloween of 1920, the night Sergeant Cronin became a victim of the times. As he left his home to start back to the barracks, a few hundred yards away, he was felled by bullets just outside his front door.

This left Mary Murphy Cronin with the burden of rearing four children: Margaret, Kathleen, James, and Patrick, the youngest not quite seven. Fortunately, the children were bright enough to win scholarships and so get an education beyond what the family income could afford. Patrick's scholarship was to St. Finian's, in Mullingar. Although the college was only twenty miles from Tullamore, he was homesick enough to feel that "from September to December was an eternity."

The boy was quite sure by now that he wanted to be a priest. The first hint of a vocation came in the seventh grade when a Jesuit, Father Saul, gave a spiritual retreat in Tullamore. Shortly after inspiring the boy to consider the Jesuits, Father Saul went as a missionary to China where he soon died of cholera.

Patrick's interest in mission work was intensified while at St. Finian's. In the college library he read the publications of the Holy Ghost fathers who were active in Africa. He also read the magazine, *African Missions,* published by the African Mission Society of Cork. His attention was diverted from Africa to the Far East when several seminarians visited St. Finian's to tell of the work the Columban Fathers were doing in China and in the Philippines.

This personal contact won out. When Patrick was graduated from St. Finian's in 1931 he sought admission to the Columban seminary at Shrule, in County Galway. The seminary was located on an old estate called Dalgan Park, 250 wooded acres along a sluggish river, a place formerly owned by an English lord who sold it when the taxes became too much for him.

The archbishop's memories of his days at Dalgan Park are happy ones. He recalls that classes were held in the elegant Georgian manor house but the students lived in four inelegant war-surplus huts bought from the British after World War I.

"It was the opposite of most seminaries today," he said. "The students lived in the middle of a large farm. Visitors were few and far between and there was plenty of quiet. We were cut off. We found there just enough hardships and just enough community spirit. It was a great place for training missionaries."

The only thing he disapproves of in his seminary training was the Holy See's stress on Latin. Philosophy and theology were taught in Latin; the Scriptures were in Latin.

"We needed more concentration on modern languages," he said. "We came out knowing English, Irish, and Latin. We should have had French or Spanish. When we attended Vatican Council II we felt handicapped by our lack of languages."

The person the archbishop remembers most clearly from his seminary days is Father Timothy Harris, the director of probationers, who left his imprint on so many future missionaries. The tall, angular ascetic had a severe look about him. One day he admonished a solemn student, "Boy, you should try to look more pleasant." The student said to Patrick Cronin, "I could have taken it from anybody else."

Father Harris lived in a vast, damp, and drafty room heated only by a turf fire at one end. To contain the heat in a small working area he surrounded himself with a warren of screens. After visiting the room a student reported, "He looks as though he is living in the middle of a *concertina.*"

In this warrenlike room the severe Father Harris gave students some of the best advice they would ever hear. For example, when a seminarian said he wanted to test his vocation, Father Harris said, "Just remember you won't be able to test it fully until the day you die. It's a day-by-day thing." He went on to explain that you don't dare separate a vocation—with all its twists and turns and burrs and briars—from the daily act of growth. Once you consider your vocation as full blown it turns artificial. A vocation, he said, can only take on a marvelous shape under the pressure of significant work.

Father Harris often stressed spiritual balance and spoke of how difficult it is to keep. He said that when you are feeling spiritually "up," enjoying spiritual consolation, that is heady wine and needs strong doses of humility for sobering purposes. This is the time to remind yourself of how weak you really are and how easily you can fall. On the other hand, when you are deep in desolation that's the time to lift your head and remind yourself that you are important because God made you, and that you are really capable of good and noble things. Spiritual balance, Father Harris felt, was especially important for a missionary.

Good grooming is something else Father Harris was a stickler about. Patrick Cronin was not. One day when Patrick, with a rip in his pants, was scrubbing the sanctuary, Father Harris came along. Patrick tried to cover the tear by squeezing his legs together, but the eagle-eyed Father Harris had seen. He pointed a finger and ordered, "Stand apart, boy!"

Father Ronan McGrath, dean of discipline, was also interested in good grooming. In those days Patrick's hair was thick and wiry and went off in all directions giving an exploding effect. With sarcasm Father McGrath said, "How do you keep your hair so tidy?" Patrick ran his hand through the disheveled mop and said, "With constant brushing, Father."

In the seminary Patrick developed a liking for athletics. He was good enough in sports to be elected captain of the swimming and the football teams. His ability came from caring. He was keyed up before every contest. One night, in his excitement before a game, he brushed his teeth with shaving cream.

"He was excited about everything he was involved in," said Father Bernard Smyth. "He got into whatever he was doing completely."

By the time Patrick Cronin was ordained, on December 21, 1937, the Columbans had extended their efforts to Korea and

Burma. So he knew the possibilities were Korea, Burma, China, or the Philippines, but he had no particular favorite, and no one asked him to make a choice. After ordination the young priests continued their studies for a few months more, until one day in the spring of 1938 appointments were posted on the bulletin board assigning Father Cronin and eight of his classmates to the Philippines.

Nearly forty years later he recalled that from that day on everything that happened in his life seemed to him something of a mystery. He cannot quite believe it. "By a series of coincidences I am in this position. It's beyond my competence and ability. And somehow I am surviving! I was only an average student. Nobody foresaw I would be put into this position. Certainly I didn't. Only through coincidence. Take for instance how I happened to be here in Cagayan de Oro: The old archbishop decided to retire. His coadjutor, with the right to succession, decided to resign at the same time. Pure coincidence!"

Patrick Cronin has found each step upward something of an embarassment. Without seeking preferment he was advanced from assistant pastor to pastor to monsignor to bishop to archbishop. At each promotion he could never quite believe it was happening. If the decisions had been left wholly to him, he would have preferred to spend his days as a pastor known only to his parishioners. He understands how the psalmist must have felt when he prayed, "Hide me in the shadow of your wings." For some reason Patrick Cronin wasn't meant to enjoy the shadows. Time and again he has been pushed into the glare of attention.

3 ✦ Strange Stirrings
in the Land

About the time Patrick Cronin was born, something remarkable was stirring in the Irish Church. Years later, Bishop Fogarty of the Diocese of Killaloe, recalled these stirrings which, at the time, had puzzled him and other bishops:

"The Spirit of God passed over Ireland in an extraordinary manner. We awoke one morning to find at our door the strangest sight imaginable—a band of young Irish priests, the finest and most gifted we had, begging! For what? That they might be allowed to go and preach the Gospel to the millions in far-off China."

Mission work in China was all that Fathers Edward Galvin and John Blowick had in mind when they founded the Columbans in 1918. They began to widen their concerns ten years later when one of their young priests, Father Hugh Sands, stopped briefly in the Philippines on his way to China. During a visit with Archbishop Michael J. O'Doherty in Manila, Father Sands was so appalled by the vastness of the prelate's problems that he wrote to the Columbans:

"The archbishop has a huge diocese—no less than two hundred parishes and not half enough priests. He has two million Catholics to look after and their condition is truly pitiable. Yesterday morning he confirmed 200 children in the parish of Santa Cruz. In that parish there is only one priest—an old man—to minister to the spiritual needs of 30,000 Catholics. Other parishes are worse. Fifty of his parishes haven't any priest. Can nothing be done for these people?"

After Father Sands had planted in the conscience of his fellow Columbans his concern for the Filipinos, the matter did not stop there. Archbishop O'Doherty continued to haunt Father O'Dwyer, the superior general of the Columbans. The archbishop simplified his needs to a point that was dramatic and graspable: "I have fifty parishes without any priest. Can you take at least one from me?"

That did it. Had he asked for dozens of priests Father O'Dwyer could, with a clear conscience, have called the request impossible. But here was an archbishop begging for only *one* priest. That was such a powerful, haunting sentence that old Columbans recall how often they quoted it at the time.

Within a year Father O'Dwyer sent three Columbans to the Philippines. The pioneers, Fathers Patrick Kelly, Michael Cuddigan and Gerald Cogan, took over the ancient parish of Malate in Manila with its 9,000 parishioners. How understaffed it was can be guessed by the fact that the 850 students in its high school were taught by only sixteen teachers. Within the parish boundaries were extremes of grandeur and poverty. Old Spanish mansions and modern apartments lined the sea front, and squalid nipa shacks huddled together in the slums around the corner.

In that year, 1929, radio was still in its infancy, especially in the Philippines, and yet the three pioneering Columbans had foresight enough to use it to reach vast numbers that they could not meet in person. Father Cuddigan wrote home: "On Sunday evening Father Kelly preached a sermon over the wireless. He felt anything but at ease beforehand, but proved quite equal to the task. When he had finished, several phone calls came through to the presbytery from appreciative listeners. Every Sunday evening a sermon is broadcast in one of the three languages—English, Spanish, and Tagalog. Learning Spanish is child's play compared with learning Tagalog."

The fact that the Columbans needed three languages to carry on their work tells something of the history of the islands. The Spanish language came with Magellan. When he discovered the archipelago, in the spring of 1521, he also brought Christianity. On Easter Sunday he invited the people to attend the first Mass ever said in the islands. After the Mass, on the island of Limasaua, the crew entertained their hosts by engaging in contests. At night they planted a cross on the island's highest hill, and, as a chronicler reported, "Each of us repeated a *pater noster* and an *ave maria.*" A few days later Magellan was killed when he allowed himself to take sides in a tribal fight on the island of Mactan.

Christianity had a more official beginning on the islands some forty years later when, in 1564, the archipelago came under Spanish rule, and was called the Philippines in honor of Philip II of Spain. The king, wishing to establish the Catholic faith there, sent six Augustinian friars. In time they were followed by Franciscans, Jesuits, Dominicans, and Recollects. These, in cooperation with Filipino priests, had made the islands predominately Catholic by 1898.

As the nineteenth century drew to a close, Filipinos began to clamor for independence. While trying to quell this rebellion, Spain was at war with the United States. The fighting came to an end when Commodore Dewey sailed into Manila Bay and sank the Spanish fleet. Spain ceded the 7,100 islands to the United States on December 10, 1898.

From that day forward the Catholic Church began to suffer setbacks. Filipinos denounced Spanish missionaries, saying they had been opposed to the nationalistic movement. More than a thousand Spanish missionaries were driven out along with any Spanish influence that could be removed. A thousand churches were left vacant because the seven hundred Filipino priests allowed to remain could not begin to care for the five million Catholics.

To compound the problem, a diocesan priest, Gregorio Aglipay, broke away from the Church to start one of his own. Fifteen other priests joined him. Their strongly nationalistic movement spread so rapidly that within a few years they numbered a million Aglipayans, members of the Philippine Independent Catholic Church.

Catholicism declined still more when the Americans brought their public school system with them. The schools were officially neutral, that is to say they were not teaching religion, and yet many teachers and supervisors were sufficiently anti-Catholic to be "neutral against" the traditional religion of their pupils.

The Catholic Church was suffering dire neglect by the time the Columbans arrived in 1929. As symbolic of the sad state of affairs, Father Arthur Price described a building in the ancient town of Binangonan, the first Columban parish outside of Manila:

"Through the open door we entered into a large cavernous hall covered with roughly hewn flagstones, well worn and dimly discernible by the aid of a solitary electric light bulb, and headed for an ancient wooden staircase in the distance. Up the creaking stairs, and we were in the main habitable part of the priest's residence known as the *convento.* Far away in one corner of the main room, the *sala,* we were able to discern the pastor of Binangonan, Father Gerald Cogan.

"The early Franciscan Friars had built well, but time and neglect had taken their toll. Actually, when Father Cogan had arrived here a couple of years previously, the *convento* was completely uninhabitable. A large tree was growing inside it. The old tin roof had disappeared. The sad state of Binangonan reflected the desolate state of many other Philippine parishes at the time."

Early in the 1930s other Columbans came to such desolation. Some went to Lingayen, a hundred miles north of Manila. Others began their work along the shores of a volcanic lake, Laguna de Bay, a few miles east of Manila. Everywhere they found ancient Spanish churches that needed rebuilding.

The towns they went to had a characteristic sameness about them. One young missionary wrote, "When you have seen one you have seen them all." He went on to say that there is always the old stone church, the public school, the market, and the municipal building with a statue of the national hero, Jose Rizal, out front. He described the large wooden houses of the rich with their corrugated iron roofs and the nipa huts of the poor, built of bamboo and thatched with palm, standing on posts four or five feet above ground. Usually there is a rickety bamboo fence. Beside the dusty road is a *sari-sari,* a store that is often an open shanty made of stray pieces of wood and enough bamboo to hold a frond roof. The proprietor often starts with a stalk of bananas and a bottle of *tuba,* a pink, foamy, inebriating fluid made from coconuts. In time he tacks a Coca Cola sign on the side of the shack and from then on is riding the heady road to capitalism.

One sight each new Columban was apt to write home about was that of the vendors carrying a basket of green eggs and shouting, *"Balut! Balut!"* A *balut* is a duck egg hatched in hot sand up to the point where the ducklings are ready to break the shell. Just before that happens the eggs are boiled—ducklings, feathers, and all—and served cold. The bravest of the new missionaries tried them. He reported that after the first traumatic tremor the delicacy was delicious.

The new priests were surprised to find a Catholic church in every town and at least a temporary chapel in most villages. In nearly every home they found a crucifix, a few holy pictures, and sometimes books of Christian doctrine. They observed that under the old order the Filipinos had absorbed external manifestations of Catholicism which are characteristically Mediterranian—statues, processions, fiestas.

In the late 1930s Patrick Cronin and his fellow seminarians at Dalgan were beginning to speak more and more about the Philippines because at that time the rest of the world was also becoming aware of the reviving Church there. This world-awareness was brought about by the opening of the 33rd International Eucharistic Congress, February 3, 1937, in Manila.

An international multitude gathered on a cool evening in Luneta park around a sanctuary luminous with floodlights and vivid with color. Half in radiance, half in shadow, sat bishops from the four corners of the earth. Below them were the white surplices and black soutanes of priests from Asia, America, Australia, Africa, and Europe. From the sanctuary steps out to the city boulevard sat pilgrims in the thousands, from the other side of the city and from the other side of the world.

Not just on the island of Luzon, the setting for the international congress, but throughout all of the islands the Church was ready to return to its high estate. Just as Archbishop O'Doherty had begged the superior general of the Columbans for priests to come to Luzon, so now Bishop James Hayes, S.J., five hundred miles to the south, was sending letters begging for priests for the diocese of Cagayan de Oro, on the island of Mindanao.

The letters and the man who wrote them gave direction to Patrick Cronin's life for the next forty years. Or as Father Harris might have said, they helped shape his vocation "under the pressure of significant work."

4 ✣ Appointment to the Philippines

During his seminary days Patrick Cronin read with care *The Far East,* the Irish edition of the magazine published by the Columbans. Through its news from the Philippines he came to learn that a *convento* is a priest's residence, a *carabao* is a water buffalo, and a *nipa* hut is thatched with fronds of nipa palms. Aside from such, his knowledge of the islands was indeed limited.

It was in 1938, a year after the Eucharistic Congress, that he was told he would be going to the Philippines along with Richard Brangan, James Corrigan, Thomas Callanan, Denis Murphy, Francis McCullagh, Martin Noone, Hugh O'Reilly—all Irishmen —and Vincent McFadden, an American, and Francis Chapman, an Australian. Assigned to lead this group was an "old China hand," Father Peter Fallon, a man destined for a martyr's death.

They were told that they would be the first Columbans to work in Mindanao.

Mindanao!

All of the articles that Patrick Cronin had read in *The Far East* had been about Luzon, the island at the top of the archipelago. The only thing he knew of Mindanao was that it is the big one at the bottom. The rest of the world probably knew even less, and yet within five years the name of Mindanao would be much repeated during the evening newscasts on radio.

By doing some quick research Patrick Cronin learned that Mindanao is about twice the size of Ireland or of Indiana. The land mass of Mindanao, however, is moulded just the opposite from the land mass of Ireland. Years after arriving in the Philippines, Father Cronin wrote: "If Ireland has been compared to a saucer with its mountains on the edge and its plains in the center, Mindanao may be compared to an inverted saucer with its mountains in the center and its plains and level areas along the coast."

The farm boys among the young Columbans were surprised to learn that a tropical island so mountainous, spiny and junglelike, and so drenched in rain could be highly agricultural. They were amazed that the coastal plains could produce such an abundance of rice, maize, coconuts, hemp, bananas, pineapples, mangoes, and other tropical fruits and vegetables. That the four surrounding seas—the Sulu, the Celebes, the Mindanao, and the Philippine— abounded in fish was something else the young priests added to the credit side in the statistics they were gathering about their future home.

They were surprised, too, in learning of the presence of Muslims on Mindanao. In the seminary they had read about Muslims, of course, but had always located them in the Middle East, never in the Philippines. Now they heard that a million Muslims—Moros, as they are called—live on Mindanao. The Moros, like most Filipinos, are a Malayan people akin to the Siamese and Javanese, having come from Malaya, the peninsula on which the port of Singapore stands.

The early settlers on Mindanao arrived by way of the island of Borneo, which is so near that it can be seen on a clear day from the southern tip of the Philippines. In Borneo they were converted to Islam during the fourteenth century. With their new religion they imbibed a warlike spirit, a spirit that would cause the Columbans trouble right up to the present.

When Spanish soldiers arrived in the sixteenth century, the Moros offered strong resistance and continued to do so through the three centuries of Spanish rule. The missionaries were no more successful in dealing with them than were the soldiers.

Their lack of success is told, in part, in the story of two Jesuits who lost their lives trying to make converts. Portraits of the Jesuits still hang on the library wall in the *convento* in Buhayen. Under one portrait is written, "He was killed by the Moros in hatred of the Faith on December 13th, 1655," and beneath the other is written, "He died with the name of Mary on his lips."

When the Jesuits returned two centuries later they enjoyed some small success, one in which crocodiles played a part. At the time of their return, 1861, the Moros were starving. They were suffering from famine, even though they had driven back into the hills two gentle native tribes, the Tiruraya and the Manobos, and had taken possession of their rich land. When the Moros were unable to feed their children they threw them to the crocodiles at the point where the Tamontaca joins the Cotabato.

An old Jesuit, Father Juanmarti, began gathering the abandoned children and caring for them. He founded an orphanage with the help of a Tiruray Christian woman. The Spanish government endowed the enterprise with a large tract of land between the rivers so that when the children grew up and married the mission was able to start them in life with a few acres. The Jesuits taught them how to till the land and supported them until they could harvest their first crop.

After the Americans took over the Philippines they succeeded where the Spanish had failed. When, in 1908, they subdued the Moros they opened the uncultivated areas of Mindanao to settlers from the overcrowded islands to the north. The Filipinos saw all of that open space and all of that rich farming country as a land of opportunity. They looked to Mindanao, as the poor of Europe had looked to America, as paradise on earth.

The new settlers came slowly at first, fearing the Moros. As the adventurous ones returned to the islands of the north with news of peace and plenty, the trickle became a flow, and finally a flood, and with this came trouble. More of that later.

The Moros were not the first settlers on Mindanao. Even before they arrived, a quiet retiring people, the Subabon, Higa-anan and the Manobos, lived on the upper slopes of the mountainous interior. They earned a bare existence from cultivating sweet potatoes and rice and from collecting rattan, a hard vine used in making wicker chairs and baskets. They were never converted to Christianity because, encircled by the Moros, they were inaccessible to Spanish missionaries.

Today they are nearly as secluded as they were forty years ago when the first group of Columbans arrived. Occasionally, these primitive people descend from their high hills and secluded valleys to buy a little salt or fish, or to sell their rattan. Even then they are cut off from the other islanders by language, for they speak a dialect of their own. Their shyness also makes their conversion a problem, and yet their peaceful ways allow missionaries to mix with them without fear of harm.

Because the Spanish had difficulties with the Muslims, a town was born on Mindanao, a town that would serve for years as the center of Columban missionary activity. The town was born when the Spanish built a line of strong forts along the northern coast of the island to keep the Moros from raiding the Christian settlements on islands to the north. Around one of these forts, the Christians developed a settlement which the Muslims referred to as Misamis, the place where Mass is offered. It was still called Misamis when the first Columbans arrived, but today it is known as Ozamis, having been renamed in honor of a prominent family in the area.

When the Columbans arrived in Mindanao they found three problems: the warlike Moros, the shy hill people, and many Christians who had not seen a priest in years. The sensible place to start was with the Christians. But before they could do that there were certain skills they had to develop.

5 ✛ Language and Horses

The newly arrived Columbans were told that while English and Spanish and Tagalog are most used, still there are at least sixty dialects spoken in the islands. Tagalog, considered the national language, is confined mainly to the Manila area and its surrounding provinces on the island of Luzon. Where the young missionaries were going, down in Mindanao, they would need Visayan, a dialect difficult for them because it has no similarity with languages of the west.

Father Cronin was sent to Cebu to live with a Filipino priest who placed him under the tutelage of an old man "more interested in learning English than in teaching me Visayan." From the old man the missionary gathered a smattering of linguistic information that did not add up to much. He learned, for example, that the passive voice is stronger than the active voice, just the opposite from English. It is more forceful to say, "You are thanked by me," than "I thank you." Knowing such nicety had little value when words and grammar were needed to build a sentence.

The most valuable thing the old man taught was the word *kwan,* an all-purpose word that translates as, "what-you-may-call-it." As verb, noun, adjective, or adverb it might seep into any phrase and may even be found several times in a sentence. When the young priest couldn't recall the proper words he could say to the houseboy, "Will you *kwan* the *kwan* because I am going to *kwan.*" The boy would saddle the horse knowing the padre was going to ride to the next village. *Kwan* could also be used to answer questions that were uncomfortable to answer. "What do you think of so-and-so?" I think he is a *kwan* man."

Sometimes the all-purpose word caused annoyance. When filling out a baptismal form, if the priest asked the mother the child's name, she might answer, "His name is *Kwan.*" After some urging she might say, Pedro. "Where was Pedro born?" "He was born in *Kwan,* padre."

Through the years Father Cronin noticed that his fellow Columbans suffered the same frustrations as he when confronted with Visayan. They were more or less pushed in and told to sink or swim. An extreme case was that of Father Oliver Whyte who upon arriving from China without a word of Visayan in his vocabulary, was told, on the first day in Mindanao, to hear confessions. He had some one write on a card: *Tolo ka maghimaya ka Maria.* So whenever there was a lull in the recitation of sins he would read the words from the card, which translate as, "Three Hail Marys."

Because of his frustrations with the language, when Patrick Cronin became bishop of Ozamis he established a language school for young missionaries. A long barracks and a few nipa huts on Iligan Bay serve as dormitories and classrooms. They are located near a rambling two-story structure, the headquarters of the Columban superior in Mindanao, a building that also serves as a rest center and a retreat house.

Newly arrived priests and nuns do six months of language study before being sent on an assignment. After a year they return for a refresher course of six weeks. They go back into the field for two more years before returning for a final six weeks at the language school.

While developing skill with the language, the Columbans were expected to develop some skill at handling horses. Patrick Cronin, as a boy on his uncle's farm in Roscommon, had ridden horses, but this had scarcely prepared him to take the swift streams and unsure mountain trails in Mindanao.

Sometimes missionaries found they had to learn to ride horses that were unwilling to be ridden. (There were enough malicious ones that horse fights were a popular sport.) Many of the animals were badly trained, if trained at all, especially those selling for a price a missionary could afford. Sometimes a young priest was expected to turn a vicious animal into a dependable mount that would cover twenty miles a day under abysmal conditions.

It was quite a sight to see a green missionary try to sit a green horse, one that reared and pawed and arched and leaped and twisted and fishtailed—anything to get shed of the unwelcome burden. Such a savage stallion unseated a Columban in a school-yard with all of the pupils looking on. The missionary recalled long afterward: "At any school in America the glee of the boys and girls would have been unconfined. They would have ribbed me no end. But the Oriental mind works differently. Without doubt my unseating was a major topic of conversation for a week. But not around me. I had "lost face." The conspiracy of silence was worse than a ribbing. Finally, the parish clerk, in trying to be kind, worked up enough courage to mention the embarrassment. He said, almost in passing, "The biology teacher suffered a similar misfortune recently."

One missionary owned a horse so vicious that the blacksmith refused to shoe the monster, summing up his feelings in a sentence: "One kick from him and you'd be praying for me all the way to the graveyard." After enduring some cajoling, the blacksmith agreed to shape the shoes on his anvil but made it clear that the padre would have to nail them on. The padre wanted to know how shoes could be shaped without trying them on and the blacksmith pointed to a patch of mud. "Let him leave his tracks there. I'll make shoes that will fit."

On the way back to his village the priest prayed that he would accomplish the job without "losing face" or the top of his head. Long afterward he said, "Those shoes, they fit like kid gloves. It wasn't difficult or dangerous. That horse seemed less concerned than the spectators who gazed in amazment from a distance. They watched me clench the nails and rasp the hooves. They had never before seen a horse with shoes. They wondered how it was possible to drive nails into a horse's legs without the animal objecting. They wondered why anyone should be foolhardy enough to go near a horse's hind legs."

When Father Cronin began traveling by horseback he found he needed to develop a new sense of timing, one that took into consideration the physical condition of the animal, the distance to be covered, the number of rivers to be crossed, the steepness of the trails, and the season of the year.

During the rainy season in Zamboanga, for instance, if the priest is due to offer Mass in a certain village on Wednesday morning, only three hours away by horseback, he still needs to leave on Tuesday morning to avoid the tropical downpour that comes in the afternoon. He must arrive before noon at a place he really doesn't have to be until the next morning. He is aware that back in his central church there is work that ought to be done, but here he sits all afternoon and evening, cooped in a tiny nipa house, looking out at the torrential rain and just waiting for time to pass.

The situation was worse when a trail led across a swamp; then a horse could not be used at all in the rainy season, so that missionaries had to travel on foot, plunging and slithering through mud as best they could. When the humidity was high and the temperature ninety in the shade, both physique and vocation were put to a test.

Father Cronin soon learned that horses are as trouble prone in Mindanao as they are anywhere else. They have to be cared for, almost like babies, or they will soon be on the sick list. Even with careful feeding and daily grooming they have a way of going lame, suffering from colic, and developing saddle sores just when they are most needed to reach an important *fiesta* three mountains away.

Horses had one great advantage, though. When a missionary got lost in the jungle, a bad situation to be in, he dropped the reins, leaned back in the saddle and gave the animal his head. Sooner or later they both reached home without a false step.

It wasn't long before all of the young missionaries began to realize the wisdom of something an old priest told them in the seminary. Upon returning from China he had said, "Develop every talent, every gift, that God has given you. You never know when it'll be needed. It doesn't make any difference what the talent is. If you have it, you have been given it because God wants you to use it. Knowing how to fix a watch for a chief in a mountain village may be the skill that leads that village to the faith."

When Father Cronin learned Visayan and horsemanship in 1938 he could not foresee how those two skills would soon save his life. Because he could understand the language and ride a horse well he would be able to escape when the Japanese began shooting at him.

6 ✢ The Pastor of Bonifacio

If the shape of Mindanao is likened to a bird in flight, at the back of the bird's head is the town of Tangub. It was there that Father Cronin had his real introduction to missionary work as assistant to his classmate, Father Francis Chapman. Father William Hennessey, an American, was also an assistant. Looking back on that year when the three of them learned the ropes together, the archbishop recalls the experience as one of the most pleasant in his life.

How surprised the three young missionaries would have been could they have foreseen the future. Father Chapman became superior of the first group of Columbans on the island of Negros and was later director of the Columban region of Australia. Father Hennessey was superior of all the Columbans in the Philippines for many years. Now the three are reunited. Fathers Chapman and Hennessey are parish priests in the Archdiocese of Cagayan de Oro.

Father Cronin arrived to find the church plaza, the heart of every Filipino town, about a half mile from Panguil Bay where fishermen lived and where hundreds of *bancas* were anchored at the shore. As he and Father Chapman walked a quarter-mile between two rows of nipa palm houses, he felt he was living inside one of the photographs in *The Far East,* the Columban fathers' magazine (now called *Columban Mission*). There was something picturesque about the way the houses were placed under the shade of coconut trees against a dense background of banana plants.

The two Columbans came upon the church in the center of the plaza, an unimposing structure devoid of architectural design and style. The only definite feature was a concrete floor. It wasn't too bad, though, they told each other. Not considering that for nearly forty years—following the expulsion of Spanish friars in 1898— Tangub had been without a resident priest. Once or twice a year an old Spanish padre had visited here. When he died in 1932 his parishioners built a church and called it San Miguel in his honor.

Father Chapman pointed above the main altar to an imposing statue of San Miguel with sword held high. Neither Columban could foresee that within less than five years the sword would disappear, stolen by Japanese soldiers, and that the church would be nearly destroyed by Japanese bombs.

The new pastor told his new assistants that, as he understood it, there were nearly fifty village chapels scattered over a parish stretching twenty-five miles along the seashore and extending deep into mountains dense with jungle. He said he had been told he had about 41,000 parishioners. Of these, 5,000 lived in the vicinity of Tangub, but most were *taga-bukids,* those living in the hill country.

It was evident to the three priests that if the parishioners could not come to town for Mass and the sacraments the priests would have to go to them, and so they developed a plan that in time became known as "doing the *barrios.* " The most thickly settled *barrios* were chosen, and arrangements made for Mass to be said there once a month on a fixed day. To some of the small *barrios* the priest went every three months. In the rest of the tiny chapels, Mass was said only on the occasion of the annual *barrio fiesta* and perhaps one other time during the year.

On a typical visit Father Cronin came riding into the *barrio* early in the evening astride a horse he now felt at home with. He visited the sick in the locality before giving instructions to children and hearing confessions. The following morning he again heard confessions and then officiated at marriages, said Mass, and administered baptism.

Before riding back to Tangub, he spent some time chatting with the people, hoping his Vasayan was improving. The parishioners were hospitable to the point of embarrassing the young missionary with their kindness. For example, in most houses there was but one bed—Filipinos usually sleep on the floor—and this was reserved for the padre.

The agreeable arrangement of the three young Columbans working together came to an end on May 1, 1940. On that day Bishop Hayes of Cagayan de Oro took away 18,000 parishioners from Tangub to establish the parish of Bonifacio, about ten miles down the road. He appointed Father Cronin as the first pastor.

The first problem was to build a church. As Archbishop Cronin observed years later, he should have started by building a house for himself. Instead, he rented a place with a galvanized iron roof, and since the landlord would not allow him to put in a ceiling the heat was unbearable. So he moved, and of this next place he wrote: "I have rented a house for $1.50 a month. It is not too bad. The boys draw the water for me from the village well. They bring it in old Socony gasoline cans. The downstairs part of the house is occupied with maize which the owner stores there. The house has only two rooms, one for the boys and one for myself. Hence my room must be my study, reception room, dining room, and bedroom, as well as my sacristy." Again he moved, this time to a remote place, so hidden that his parishioners kept complaining that they could not find him. Then he moved into a bungalow right downtown, a place so attractive to God's little creatures that Patrick Cronin awakened each night aware of things walking over him. As a result of this unpleasant housing experience the archbishop always advises his young priests to build first a house for themselves and then start to work on the church.

What he used as a church at first was a roof, supported by eight wooden posts, and sides made from palm leaf thatch. The altar was a few common boards nailed together. No floor, no windows, no doors, no pews, no confessional, no sacristy. Everything was falling down.

"I brought my Mass kit with me from Tangub," he wrote, "and that is about all the parish has in church furniture. I must keep my vestments and altar equipment in the house. I have no tabernacle and anyhow I could not dream of keeping the Blessed Sacrament in the shed that now serves as a church.

"The day-long absence of the Blessed Sacrament means a big spiritual loss for my people as well as for myself. Further, it means an additional physical burden for the priest, because every sick call involves making two journeys. Not having the Blessed Sacrament reserved, I cannot bring Holy Viaticum to the sick person on my first visit. I must return the following morning after Mass. This often entails a long journey on horseback."

He said that in those days he used to dream of a church complete with tabernacle, confessional, crucifixes, altar cloths, a ciborium, a monstrance, a missal, a vestment press, a harmonium. That doesn't seem like much to ask for in most places, but it seemed an awful lot to dream of in Mindanao.

Father Cronin bought four acres in the middle of Bonafacio and built a wooden church and a school. He felt he needed the school because while "doing the *barrios*" was important, even more important was religious instruction of children. The hope of the church in Mindanao was with the children; so many adults were numbed with indifference after forty years of being without a priest. They had the faith all right, the young pastor admitted, but it was what the theologians call "the habit of faith," and not its practical exercise.

Trying to teach religion in the public schools was an exercise in untangling red tape. It could be taught in a school building three half-hour periods a week outside of school hours. Written permission from the parents had to be obtained. These and other conditions made the young missionary decide he could do better with schools of his own.

Even if he had the schools he could not begin to teach all of the religion courses. He needed catechists, and so he turned to some bright young women who were willing to help. Some were well trained, having attended Catholic high schools, but most needed instruction themselves.

About that time Bishop Hayes arranged for a catechetical institute to be held in the town of Misamis. The pastors of the area sent in nearly 200 would-be catechists. The institute, conducted by two veteran missionaries, one Dutch and one Filipino, was too brief in duration, but at least it was a start. Father Cronin had a feeling that some seeds had been planted from which good things might grow.

7 ✛ Everywhere Fiestas

Patrick Cronin realized early in his apostolate that if he was to be "all things to all men" he would have to be sensitive to local cultures and customs. He learned this lesson so well that years later a young missionary remarked, "We say around here that when it comes to understanding the Filipinos, Archbishop Cronin is endowed with infallibility."

One of the first things learned was that at any large function it is not proper for the priest to thank his host and hostess and depart. He must proceed on a formal visit to every room, announcing at each, "I am going now," for it is considered most impolite to leave a gathering without first informing everyone.

Father Cronin soon decided that at a funeral the priest must resign himself to the marching band. A Columban learned the importance of this when he asked a family why they didn't call a doctor or buy some medicine for their sick granny, and was told they were saving the money to have the funeral. The priest recalls that at the graveside the band played, "It Had to be You."

And then there is the *fiesta* to honor the patron saint of the village. This blending of the sacred and the secular puts heavy demands on a priest's time and energy, but he must learn to accept it with good grace. Father Cronin lived through many *fiestas* each year because many *barrios* were under his spiritual direction.

Usually it began when a *barrio* chief visited the young pastor to announce the date and observe, "It will be a *bibo* (lively) *fiesta*, Padre. We not had the Mass for one year already. Will be *daghan kasals, daghan bunyag. Bibo kaaya,* Padre." When translated it means a lot of work for the priest—many marriages, many baptisms, a lively *fiesta.*

For all its air of giddy carnival, the *fiesta* is primarily a religious event. It begins with a novena in preparation for the feast. Each evening for nine evenings the people gather in their little chapel where one of them, almost always an older woman, leads the community in prayer.

Usually on the last evening before the great day Father Cronin arrived on horseback, by foot, or by boat, depending on the location of the village. First he visited his host's house to have a quick meal and to meet the committee: One member had seen to hanging bunting in the streets, another to hiring a band, and another to raising funds.

Often the fund raiser was in charge of electing the queen around whom all festivities swirled. The queen was chosen from among the prettiest girls in the *barrio,* with fund-raising in mind. The young men of property were enticed to invest in votes—say, one vote, one *centavo.* A foolish gallant might sell his only *carabao* to set his beloved upon the great carved chair. The money thus realized went to pay the expenses of the *fiesta.*

At sunset Father Cronin would walk to the chapel, passing beneath colored pieces of paper and crepe that rustled festively from wires stretched across the street. The band, parading up and down, played schmaltzy tunes.

Confessions, after going on and on, were followed by instructions of the dozen or so couples who hoped to be married the next morning. After leading the closing of the novena, with the band performing in the center of the church, Father Cronin again heard confessions, this time late into the night.

After midnight he stretched out on a board bed or a straw mat, exhausted enough to ignore the noises of the night. He didn't hear women calling to each other as they worked late making sweet-milk candies and puddings from coconut juice and yellow corn. He wasn't bothered by pigs squealing, hens squawking, and geese hissing their final act of defiance. And usually not until the next day did he learn that some men had tried out the fireworks to see if they would be effective for the feast.

Mass was scheduled for seven, but *fiesta* Masses nearly always started two hours late. First came the weddings, the shy couples awkward in their unaccustomed outfits. Father Cronin marveled at the beautiful white gowns, spotless despite rain and mud.

Most of the couples standing before him had been brought together through the ministrations of a matchmaker. The pairings were arrived at only after hours of discussing terms of the marriage, which included the *bugay,* or bride price, the gift given to the girl's father for the loss of a helper. The gift might include two acres of land, a water buffalo, 500 ears of corn, a Mass offered for the girl's deceased relatives, a pig and a cow, enough *tuba* to drink at the wedding feast, and the bride's apparel—veil, dress, ring, earrings, and necklace.

During the ceremony the bride had custody of the rings and coins, symbols of fidelity and the completion of the marriage contract. If she dropped a coin it was regarded as a sign of bad luck, and if her veil fell off it was a sign of sorrow, or even death.

The saying is that the one who holds the candle higher or who stands first after Mass will run the family. To strengthen this hold one must step on the other's feet. Such maneuvering was watched closely by relatives.

If rain was beating down, as is often the case so near the equator, it was considered a promise of fertility. Judging from all of the children in the congregation there were many rainy wedding days in the past.

After Mass came a short procession around the village. A rudely carved statue of the patron saint, highly colored, was the center of attention. The queen and the band were also much in evidence.

Then the baptisms began. The service was delayed until certificates could be completed, a slow process because of the names some of the parents were wishing on their offspring. Father Cronin tried to explain that the names should be those of saints. He must not have been persuasive in all cases because years later Father Edward De Persio sat on the verandah in Bonifacio and listed the names of children in the local school. For boys he wrote down Hermogenes, Dionesio, Candido, Teotimo and Lucipero. Among the girls were Primativa, Altagracia, Luzviminda, Iluminda and Placrista. He especially liked Genesis and expected at any time to come across Apocalypso.

Nicknames were often requested. Pearly Shells and Pee Wee seemed popular. One sponsor, married for fifteen years, had to ask her husband his real name for the baptismal certificate.

Father James Moynihan is still puzzled as to how three sons

were named Edgar and Allen and Poe when neither parent spoke or read English. Many of the babies, however, were given the most Christian names in the calendar: there were Chrysostoms, Gregorys, Cyprians, Agathas, and Perpetuas to no end. The scene became lively when a "Greek Father" got out of hand at his first taste of salt and a "Roman martyr" protested vehemently when strangled by a clumsy sponsor.

The first thirty wailing and cooing babies were no sooner made Christians than forty-five more were ready. Then twenty-five more came screaming and smiling. This was followed by a break for something to eat. Chicken livers, roast ribs, cattle marrow, fish roe, and rich custards of all kinds.

Perhaps twenty more infants would be ready after lunch. Then a long wait to be sure the late arrivals would be taken care of. Finally twenty-five more received the waters. By the end of the day Father Cronin might find himself with a bundle of 150 baptismal certificates tucked into his saddle bags, a not unusual number in those early days.

By now the men of the village had seen enough of religious ceremonies, had used up the fireworks, and were bored with the repetitious band. So they turned to their favorite pastime— cockfighting. At the first sounds from the cockpit, Father Cronin reminded himself that on the way back to Bonifacio, he should try to avoid any man carrying a rooster. It is considered bad luck to pass too close to a priest on the way to a fight.

By this time the bridal couples had departed with relatives and friends. In the mountain areas a *balsa* (bamboo sled) drawn by a *carabao* was sometimes used as a taxi, more often everybody walked with a band—two guitars and two banjos—playing happy music along the trails.

At the bride's house the couple was met at the door by an elderly relative who gave them a cool glass of water from which both drank. Often they broke the glass to signify oneness and stressing the fact that the vessel the couple share will never be used by another. Rice was thrown to express a wish for fertility and the couple's hair combed to insure a peaceful and orderly wedded life.

The newlyweds entered a room where an altar had been prepared. They knelt holding lighted candles while the father and the mother of the bride gave a long sermon on the duties of married life, while relatives sighed and sobbed. The couple arose to kiss the hands of their parents and the white veil was removed from the bride's head.

By the time Father Cronin started back to Bonifacio, wedding feasts were in full flight all through the hills. The newlyweds opened the feast by eating from the same plate, a sign of perfect sharing. If a plate broke during the time of feasting it was considered a sign of good luck. There was an abundance of rice, beef, pork, chicken, goat, and plenty of *tuba.*

After the feasting, the dancing began. Each dancer tossed coins in a plate at the bride's feet. When the couple placed a mat on the floor they were showered with money as they danced. Finally the parents offered a going away gift: the promise of a new house, a *carabao,* or a shelf of jars filled with rice, corn, and salt.

Father Cronin was usually back in his *convento* in Bonifacio long before the wedding guests quit dancing and *fiesta* celebrants collapsed amid the shambles. He never saw the limp buntings waiting for the wind and rain to bring them down. Already he was consulting his calendar, aware that even now bands were forming for other *fiestas* in other villages.

8 ✢ Customs Galore

While *fiestas* of patron saints were numerous, at least they were scattered throughout the year. The big problems were the feasts of All Souls, Christmas, and Easter because each was celebrated in all villages at the same time. Each village wanted the padre to perform its religious services and to be the important guest at social functions.

The "important guest" looms large in the Filipino's consciousness. In the honorific seating arrangements at table, the doctor outranks the teacher because he has spent more years in school and displays a more formidable diploma, but the man of the cloth is the most important guest at every function no matter how trivial.

If he had to name one day of the year as the busiest, Father Cronin would probably have said it was All Souls' Day. Preparation for the feast started early in October when groups went from house to house singing ballads, pleading that the dead be remembered.

In country villages the custom was to erect a small chapel where each October evening the local musicians joined the parishioners in singing the rosary in Spanish. Since they no longer understood Spanish, one Columban thought it might be more devout if they prayed in the local dialect. The parishioners agreed and said the rosary with him. When they had finished they began the whole thing all over in Spanish, with musical accompaniment. At that instant the Columban learned, what every missionary must, the power of tradition.

On the eve of All Souls, people dressed in their finest, flocked to the cemetery well supplied with food. Candles flickered in the darkness and shadows glided from group to group.

For two days, from dawn of All Saints until dark of All Souls, Father Cronin, accompanied by acolytes and choir girls, moved from grave to grave, blessing each according to the custom. A big umbrella atop a tall pole shaded the group from the blazing heat. The aroma of incense hung on the sultry air and the chant of the choir seemed unending.

Gifts to the departed were displayed atop many graves. On a child's were cookies and colorful paper flowers; on an old tippler's, a pack of cigarettes and two open bottles of San Miguel beer.

Young Father Cronin felt uneasy when first he heard that graves are exhumed periodically and the remains transferred to a central common plot over which towers a great cross. This frees the individual graves for future use by the family. As a result, bones and parts of skulls may turn up while relatives are dressing the grave. The naturalness with which these bits and pieces are rearranged startles someone from a western culture where the naturalness of death is not taken so for granted.

For two days the priest and his little cluster of assistants trudged back and forth and up one hill and down another in as many cemeteries as they could reach. Under the shade of coconut groves, families sat for hours waiting with the patience of the East for the graves of their relatives to be blessed. Even the children, usually frisky, were strangely quiet. With large agate eyes, they paused in the presence of a great mystery: "It is appointed to man once to die."

Christmas in Mindanao is a three-week celebration. That was some help because it gave Father Cronin nine days before the great feast and twelve after it to visit numerous *barrios.*

The celebration started at about 3:30 on the morning of December 16 with the sacristan vigorously ringing the church bell while a local band marched through the town and the houseboy sent up a rocket. As the pastor hurried through the night to the confessional he noticed the church was beginning to fill; more people would be there today than on most Sundays.

Many were from *barrios* scattered through the mountains. For those unable to make the trip and too far away to hear the bells, the rocket in the sky told them that Mass was about to begin. The Mass of the Cock's Crow *(Misa del Gallo)* started about four o'clock because tradition dictated that it must end before morning's first light.

Right after Mass the children, and some adults, returned to the

pleasant task of making Christmas decorations. The most important were the *bito-on* (star) and the *parol* (lantern). The custom
of celebrating Christmas with lanterns dates back to 1882, when,
two weeks before the feast, the townspeople put up arches hung
with lanterns. On the day before the *Misa del Gallo,* the town crier
made the rounds to remind people to hang lanterns in windows
or doorways so that the road to church would be brightly lit for
all. What started as a practical measure became a tradition. In
time the lantern shaped like a star became the Filipino symbol for
Christmas.

Since Mindanao is too hot for growing Christmas trees the
children made their own. They covered the dense twigs of a dead
branch with tiny bits of paper to give the effect of snow, something
they had never seen. This they mounted in a sand box and added
colorful decorations, mostly in the shape of bells.

Each day before dawn Father Cronin said a Mass, a traditional
preparation for the great event celebrated at Midnight Mass on
Christmas Eve. That night during the *Gloria,* while church bells
pealed, every head in the congregation turned to look up to the
choir loft. A yellow paper star, with a candle inside, came gliding
in a jerky descent down a long wire until it stood above the crib
near the altar.

After Midnight Mass Father Cronin tried to get some sleep
before the regular morning Masses. But throughout Bonifacio
much was happening. First there was a midnight supper at which
rice dishes and coconut candy were the delicacies. Afterward the
children kissed their parents' hands, an old Spanish tradition, and
hurried off in search of godparents who were expected to give gifts.
Then came the fireworks. Through it all the band played on.

The celebrations ended January 6, the Feast of the Three Kings.
Once more at the *Gloria* the star was put in motion. Little by little
it returned to the upper reaches of the church signifying it had
shown three kings the way and so fulfilled its destiny.

In Holy Week the activities began on Spy Wednesday when
Father Cronin entered the confessional. Many parishioners had
come to Bonifacio from outlying *barrios* to spend the week with
relatives and friends. For them this was a time to fulfill the Easter
obligation by going to confession and receiving communion.

Since Father Cronin was the only priest in a parish of 18,000 souls, the burden of the confessional was great but not so great as the number suggests. Many had stayed away from the sacrament for years and did not know how to approach it. Or were ashamed to.

While the priest was in the confessional, parishioners descended on the church to scrub and sweep with vigor and to discuss at length on how to best prepare the statues for various processions. This went on until the office of *Tenebrae* was recited from six until nearly eight o'clock. Afterward the pastor was kept busy for hours answering questions and receiving the hill people who wanted to recall how they had met their padre at a *fiesta* in some remote *barrio*.

Before the first cock got around to crowing on Holy Thursday, Father Cronin was back in the confessional. Mass began at 7:30, followed by a procession of the Blessed Sacrament to the altar of repose. Three times the procession halted and each time the congregation bowed low in adoration as the censer swung in fragrant arcs.

The mandatum of the Holy Week ritual, known as *paghugas* in Visayan, was performed in the afternoon when the pastor washed the feet of twelve acolytes, dressed in flowing robes, representing the twelve apostles. After the ceremony the *presidenta* of the town treated the apostles to a dinner in memory of the Last Supper.

That evening Father Cronin conducted another *Tenebrae* service, and once more spent a couple of hours in the confessional. Through the night, men of the parish formed a guard of honor keeping watch at the altar of repose.

Ceremonies for Good Friday began at 7:30 in the morning. At the "Adoration of the Cross," the entire congregation approached to kiss the crucifix. Father Cronin thought the stream of people would never end. In the afternoon the Way of the Cross was held out of doors where a crowd accompanied its pastor as he retraced the sorrowful journey to Calvary. The lamentations of the old women were poignant; they reminded the young priest of the "keening" over the dead in Ireland.

When night came down suddenly, as it does in the tropics, the ceremony called *paglubong,* the burial of Christ, began. Father

Cronin wearing surplice, black stole, and cape, took his place behind the bier. As the procession moved through the dark and quiet town, the only sound was that of the funeral marches played by the band. An hour later the procession arrived back at the church.

After a hurried dinner the pastor returned to the confessional where he remained well into the night.

But the day wasn't over. Another procession awaited his presence. At ten o'clock the *Soledad* began. The idea is that Mary, distracted by grief, leaves her house and wanders through the streets of Jerusalem seeking her son. The statue of Our Lady draped in black was carried through town accompanied by women carrying candles past houses illuminated with dozens of lights. The silence and peace of the tropical darkness was unbroken as the procession continued until nearly midnight.

Father Cronin spent most of Holy Saturday hearing confessions, and he was back in the confessional by four o'clock Easter morning. At five o'clock began the procession called the *pagtagbo,* a commemoration of the meeting of Christ and his mother. Men carrying a statue of Christ moved in one direction while women carrying one of Mary moved in the opposite direction. Eventually they met in front of an elevated platform at the church, a platform brilliantly illuminated because daybreak had not yet come.

On the ground stood four girls dressed as angels complete with wings. On the platform above were two more angels hidden from sight. After the meeting of Jesus and Mary, a curtain was drawn aside and the two angels were slowly lowered. They descended singing *Regina coeli, laetare alleluia,* while the four angels below joined in harmony.

Upon reaching the statue of Our Lady, one angel removed the black veil and replaced it with one of gleaming white, and the second angel set a crown on the head. Having fulfilled their destiny both ascended to the place from which they had come.

Finally the Mass of Easter morning. It was a sung Mass. During it the young pastor gave out communion to a throng consoling in its numbers. A memorable ending to a week that left him grateful, happy, and ready to sleep around the clock.

The pastor of Bonifacio soon learned that besides official feasts there were other days marked for religious observance. Of all these local celebrations he found the *Flores de Mayo,* the Flowers of May, the most delightful.

On his first May Day in Bonifacio, while walking along the town's dusty street, the new pastor came upon Teresita leading her wide-eyed brother with one hand and clutching a bunch of wilted pink and white flowers with the other. Teresita greeted Father Cronin with, "Good afternoon, Fadder. We are going to the *Flores.*" Her cousins Carmen and Rudolpho were also going to the *Flores,* she said, as were all those other children moving in groups of twos and threes toward the church plaza.

The *Flores,* daily devotions to Mary during May, combined instruction with piety. First the children gathered in the church for lessons in Christian doctrine and prayer. Before long the wooden structure shook with chirrup and chatter. Girl catechists were in charge. These same girls had earlier visited the nipa houses under the palm streets persuading mothers to send the children.

Some of the offbeat answers that came from catechism classes in Mindanao were delightful. For example, when a catechist asked, "Will you tell me, Jose, what we must do before we can be forgiven?" the boy answered, "First we must sin."

In describing what happened at the wedding feast of Cana, Romeo Roa said, "Jesus said to Mary, 'What does it matter, *we* have *ours.*'"

In the interval, from the time the catechism classes were dismissed until the ceremony of the *Flores* began, Father Cronin watched the children playing outside the church. Most were poorly clad but always clean. As they buzzed around like bees at a hive, eight little girls stood out demurely from the rest. They wore spotless white dresses and veils. Tomorrow they will be as simply and poorly dressed as the rest, but this afternoon they will have the honor of carrying the eight festooned standards, each with a large white letter printed on it. Two other girls, with wreaths around their heads and wings on their shoulders, waited at the church door. These angels would escort the standard bearers to the sanctuary. The other children paused in their flight from time to time to admire the glory of their friends. Before the month is over each will have had a chance to play this part for a day.

The girl with the standard bearing a large A, accompanied by the two solemn angels, walked slowly up to the altar, put the standard in position, and walked gravely back. Then came the girl with the letter V and, on and on, until eight standards were in position spelling AVE MARIA before the statue of Our Lady.

All the children came forward bearing flowers toward the altar. They sang a hymn and as they finished threw the flowers at the statue. The *Flores* was over for another day and soon the church was quiet. As the young pastor entered to read his breviary, flowers and petals were thick on the sanctuary floor and the air was heavy with a spring sweetness.

At such times Patrick Cronin was aware of the differences between here and home. He had been accustomed to the restrained and unembellished observances in Ireland. Such blandness was unthinkable in Bonifacio.

9 ✢ War's Horror

Just as Father Cronin was beginning to feel at home with Filipino customs the world turned topsy-turvy. On the Feast of the Immaculate Conception, December 8, he came out of church to hear his excited parishioners repeating one name over and over: Pearl Harbor! The Japanese will invade Mindanao at any time, they said, and their young pastor feared they were right.

The first sign of war came when crippled American planes, held together by little more than hope, landed on and took off from the airfield owned by the Del Monte plantation in the Bukidnon mountains, just above Cagayan de Oro. In the middle of March of 1942 General MacArthur, having been ordered by President Roosevelt to leave Corregidor, arrived in Mindanao by PT boat with his wife and son. From the airfield at Del Monte the MacArthurs flew to Australia.

The long drought and oppressive heat of May 1942 were bad enough, but the news was worse. The Columbans tried to cheer each other with the nightly reports that Corregidor was holding out. But they knew that artillery was pounding the big rock from Bataan and Cavite and that enemy bombers could do their work at will without any fear of antiaircraft guns.

By May the Japanese forces were closing in on Mindanao. Their shipping greatly increased in the Visayan Sea. They overran Cebu about the time American troops were retreating into the mountains in Panay. Soon the enemy landed in the province of Davao, on the southern coast of Mindanao, and fanned out while moving northward. Everyone was getting the feeling of being trapped.

When the Japanese reached the Province of Misamis Occidental (now Ozamis) the governor surrendered immediately. When Cagayan de Oro was surrendered, Bishop Hayes was put into a concentration camp where he was given the job of porter.

Everything went so smoothly that the invaders, lulled into a false sense of security, scarcely manned the old Spanish fortress in Misamis. The first warning that the Japanese had of impending danger came from the ragtag army of Captain Luis Morgan, a *mestizo* with an American father and a Filipina mother. Before the war Luis Morgan, sometimes called William, was a junior lieutenant in the Philippine Constabulary. Even then he was considered a swaggering Rudolph Valentino, especially by the village girls. No sooner had the war broken out when he promoted himself to captain and collected under his command four hundred Filipino soldiers.

"Morgan was a daredevil," said Archbishop Cronin recalling the war thirty-five years after the event. "One night he crossed the bay and attacked the Spanish fortress and found only three Japanese civilians there. He killed them. I said at the time that this was unnecessary and that the Japanese would make the Filipinos pay for it a hundredfold. At the fortress, Morgan freed four Filipinos who had been arrested for robbing a Chinese merchant. Two of them joined his forces and the other two went off to celebrate."

The first wave of Japanese on Mindanao were crack troops, real professionals. They did their work and moved on to fight on other islands in the South Pacific. What came now were the dregs of the Japanese army.

They lived off the land so effectively that a Filipino farmer complained, "Before war we fat hog today so we can die hog tomorrow. Now can't fat hog. No hog. Work he is so many; chow she is so few."

He was feeling the oppression of the invaders who forced Filipino farmers to harvest all rice, corn, bananas, and coconuts for them. The troops lived off the land completely and shipped the surplus to Tokyo. Whatever remained they destroyed in hopes of starving the islanders into submission.

To pass through a village after the invader had abandoned it was an uneasy experience. Half-eaten animals and fowls lay rotting in the tropical sun, and the stench, flies, and fierce red ants were appalling. To add to the horror, a plague of rats and of seven-year locusts blighted the land.

The habit that the Japanese had of soaking in scalding baths caused almost as much destruction as their heavy weapons because they tore down houses to get fuel to heat water. To build a funeral pyre for their dead they used furniture.

"Fathers Chapman, Hennessey, and I took to the hills," said Archbishop Cronin. "We hid at the foot of Mount Malindong, the third largest mountain in the Philippines. Seven thousand feet high. In the dark forest and deep valleys an army could escape detection."

Even the Columbans, already accustomed to living in austere *conventos* cared for by careless houseboys, became aware of the new sparseness. When they got together they recalled as pleasant memories such small luxuries as razor blades, shoe laces, soap, toothpaste, cigarettes, needles, thread, socks, shoes, sugar, salt, matches, and medicine.

The lack of medicine was serious because of frequent attacks of dysentery and malaria. The home remedy for dysentery was a strict diet of baked *camotes* (sweet potatoes). For malaria cinchona bark was converted into quinine.

The archbishop recalls that he learned from his parishioners how to make do. One of the most important things they taught him was how to start a fire by rubbing together two pieces of bamboo in a certain way. This was helpful because the guerrillas were using all available kitchen matches as percussion caps for rifle ammunition; the shells were segments of curtain rods stuffed with dynamite, amatol, and firecracker powder; lead bullets were fashioned from fishermen's sinkers. Needless to say the rifles often blew sky high.

The Filipinos in the hills also knew how to use tough vines for shoestrings and how to carve buttons from coconut shells. They made lamps by pouring coconut oil into broken bottles and devised drinking cups from bamboo tubes. Clothing was woven from hemp fiber and effective rainwear was fashioned from banana leaves six feet long and three feet wide.

Although they were not threatened by starvation, the food they had was often unsavory. An American told of the time he dined in the hills with a Moro whose sullen young wife did not want to prepare the meal. She thrust at him a filthy pot that gave off a gamey stench. It was filled with ill-cooked brown mountain rice in which nestled little legs, arms, and hands. Monkey.

The Columbans warned each other to be wary of "self-supporting" pigs, for they were supposed to carry dysentery and cholera. A self-supporting pig was one not fed by its owner but allowed to roam, getting food from outhouses.

The missionaries found the terrain especially inhospitable after leaving the main roads to move into unfamiliar mountains. Getting lost in the jungle is always a danger, especially when trying to avoid an enemy patrol, or when taking a short cut to bypass a dense tangle. Suddenly you are going in the wrong direction. To get turned around is so easy when visibility is limited to a few yards and when everything is so repetitious that reference points are impossible to find. Everybody soon learned that the best piece of advice is the oft-repeated admonition: stick to the trails.

Even on the trails the Columbans found themselves moving through a forest that burdened them with tropical heaviness and intolerable annoyances. Leeches started tropical ulcers; vines caused itching; burning mosquito bites turned the face into a swollen welt. There was slimy water to wade through and the irritating chatter of monkeys to put up with. This was no tropical paradise.

But this is getting ahead of the story. Before leaving Bonifacio for the mountains Father Cronin had come to know Colonel Wendell Fertig, an American who would soon become a legend in the Philippines. It was Colonel Fertig who sent the young pastor hurrying to the hills when he came running into the *convento* at midnight saying, "The Japs have landed and are coming up the road fast. You better clear out."

Earlier in the day the colonel had said, "The jungle is bad and no place for any man, but it is to be preferred to the Japs."

Morgan's men were vexing the enemy and the enemy was retaliating. The guerrillas, for instance, dug trenches in the road and covered them with bamboo and a thin coat of dirt; trucks crashed through and overturned. Above mountain roads they carefully balanced rocks, using them to start avalanches to engulf convoys and marching troops. They planted in the trail sharp pieces of short bamboo to pierce the feet of the unwary.

The Japanese tried to stop this with atrocities. One sentence in the diary of Father Edward Haggerty, S.J., tells enough of the chilly story: "Near Imbatug I buried people sawed in two."

10 ✢ Guerrillas Get a Leader

ertig had been a rumor well before Father Cronin met him. That is how it was, everybody and everything that did not fit the prevailing pattern became a rumor. All news was reduced to gossip that flew swiftly from mouth to ear, as the Filipinos say, a form of communication known as the bamboo telegraph.

Years later Father Cronin wrote in the old Columban magazine, *The Far East,* about the day he met Colonel Wendell Fertig: "The monsoon rains had brought life and growth to the countryside, but few people had time to watch the dark green of the corn on the upland hills or the bowed heads of the waving rice in the paddy fields. All minds were focused on the disastrous course of the war and on their personal problems. There was no hope for immediate assistance and some began to doubt the ultimate victory of the Allies. I was wondering how these things might affect myself and the work I was engaged in."

A few months earlier people had said that the Philippines would be liberated by Christmas. Rumors of a great American fleet steaming toward Mindanao had sped across the bamboo telegraph. But now happy rumors were few, and Father Cronin, who also had a large investment in hope, slowly resigned himself to a long and dreary war.

Such solemn thoughts were shattered when an excited parishioner came running up the steps of the verandah shouting that Colonel Fertig was on his way. Minutes later the colonel stood framed in the doorway. His khakis seemed more starched than they really were because he stood straight and tall. As Father Cronin stepped onto the verandah he observed that his guest had close-cropped sandy hair and a neatly trimmed red goatee.

Years later Patrick Cronin recalled, "He greeted me with a warm handshake and said, 'Don't let things get you down, Father.' "

The priest looked forward to the colonel's visits. Night after night they sat in rattan chairs on the verandah, surrounded by heavy heat, chirring locusts, banana groves, coconut trees, and the densely jungled hills. During the conversation the colonel paused from time to time to rub his lips with coconut oil, which he carried in a small vial, hoping to relieve their dry, chapped condition; he was paying the price of blondness in the tropics.

As a United States Army engineer, Fertig had operated mining camps in the Philippines for five years before the war. After escaping death on the plains on Luzon, in the Bataan jungles, and on the desolate rockiness of Corregidor, he felt he had been spared for a special assignment. This sense of mission was more easily admitted to a priest than to his fellow soldiers.

The colonel told the young pastor that he had been ordered out of Corregidor to join General MacArthur's headquarters in Australia. The first airplane that was to lift him from the Rock crashed on landing there. He boarded the second and escaped uninjured when it crashed on take off. Through a confusion of orders he missed the submarine that was to evacuate him. He finally escaped on the last navy flying boat to leave Corregidor before the surrender. He never reached Australia, though, because the flying boat crashed on Lake Lanao in Mindanao.

Father Cronin must have wondered how Fertig felt about Divine Providence. He had no way of knowing that the colonel had written in his diary: "God, you've helped me this far. Thank you for your help. I'll try to do the best I can, and I hope you'll want to go on helping me. God, if it is my fate to tell other people what to do, please help me to guess right."

Much later he wrote: "During the months in the forest, I have become acquainted with myself and developed a feeling that I do not walk alone; a feeling that a Power greater than any human power has my destiny in hand. Like a swimmer, carried forward by a powerful current, I can direct my course as long as my way lies in the direction of the irresistible flow of events. Never have I lost the feeling that my actions have followed a course plotted by some Power greater than any human agency."

Eventually, when things were going badly for the guerrillas, Fertig's prayer was the same each night: "God, give us time."

During Fertig's early talks with Father Cronin the name of Luis

Morgan, the guerrilla leader, haunted the conversation. The colonel complained that Morgan was creating ill will for the allied cause. For one thing, he demanded taxes and threw into concentration camps anyone he thought ought to be there. The rumors of his atrocities were many. On one occasion he was said to have wiped out every man, woman, and child in a Moro village as reprisal for some murders committed by marauding Moros. The people who once said, "If a man is brave, and has a gun, he joins Morgan" were not saying it any more.

And then the miracle happened. Morgan asked Fertig to take control of his army. By now Morgan had 600 riflemen armed with machine guns and automatic rifles and 60,000 rounds of ammunition. Fertig suspected there must be a catch in this sudden surge of generosity, and so there was.

Former Philippine Army officers, the sons of illustrious families, were scheming to bring the many guerrilla movements together into a more effective unit. Morgan knew that when this happened he would be outside looking in. If, however, Colonel Fertig assumed command of all guerrillas and made Morgan his second-in-command he could still play the role of swashbuckling soldier of fortune so admired by the village girls.

Fertig was a friend of Father Thomas Callanan, a man of sparkling courtesy, who had come to Mindanao with Patrick Cronin. The colonel said in the book, *They Fought Alone,* that Father Callanan had something to do with his decision to become the guerrilla leader of the island. When he asked Father Callanan if he could depend on the support of the Church, the young pastor of Jimenez explained that officially the Church was neutral, but that unofficially it was at war with the Japanese because they said that they intended to drive the American and all of his beliefs from East Asia. A Japanese official had boasted to a Filipino priest, "No more Jesus Christ. All now belong Nippon."

One night Father Callanan and Fertig were guests at a dinner party given by the leading political family of Mindanao, the Ozamis family of Jimenez. When Dona Carmen, the head of the house, spoke of the guerrilla movement she looked carefully at Father Callanan. Fertig always believed that she gave her approval after she saw that the Columban was at least not opposed to the movement. The colonel said later that the real guerrilla movement was born that night in the Casa Ozamis. The feeling that he had the tacit approval of the missionaries gave him the courage to follow, as he wrote in his diary, "a course plotted by some Power greater than any human agency."

Thirty-five years later, Father Callanan, still in Mindanao, said, "The American guerrillas couldn't understand the missionaries. At least not at first. They were puzzled about why we were here. They saw girls around the *barrios* and supposed that we kept a harem. But after living with us for a time they saw that this was not the case. The soldiers hung around us and had to live on our terms. We kept them out of trouble and they began to see that that is a good way to live."

The Americans that Father Callanan spoke of were some of the 200 who had escaped Japanese internment. These were the men Colonel Fertig used to help him form an army of 35,000 Filipinos. When leaders of seventy resistance units were offered a chance to unite under Fertig, some accepted readily, some sneered, and many took a wait-and-see attitude.

To gain the prestige he needed to be accepted as The One, Fertig promoted himself to the rank of major general. To make it look official, even if it wasn't, he asked a Moro silversmith to hammer out some silver stars.

Morgan, as second in command, never ceased to be a problem. He was on the verge of mutiny more than once. Eventually Fertig told Morgan he was sending him to Australia to serve as an advisor on General MacArthur's staff. After radioing ahead that Morgan was a troublemaker he received a radio message saying to keep him in Mindanao. Fertig ignored the message and sent the problem child anyway, later telling MacArthur's staff that the message had arrived too late.

11 ✛ Contact with Australia

W hile in hiding, the Columbans conducted services in chapels built without nails or wood, fragile structures with
sides of bamboo and roofs of nipa fronds. The holy water
fonts were usually coconuts cut in two. Some priests said Mass
only once a week because host flour and Mass wine were scarce.

No matter how deep they moved into the hills, they found the
familiar odor of Southeast Asia permeating even the smallest
village—food frying in coconut oil, charcoal smoke, and flowers.
Also as ubiquitous as the very air were the Volunteer Guards, a
group of civilians who protected the trails, acted as guides and
couriers, and transported food and baggage. Sometimes, armed
with heavy knives called *bolos,* they joined the guerrillas in a night
ambush.

All of this drama and danger brought Father Cronin and his
parishioners closer together. The pastor went about visiting their
homes set against betel palm, jackfruit trees, and slender mountain
bamboo. Besides speaking of God, he spent much time listening
to talk that had come across the bamboo telegraph, a blending of
propaganda, rumor, and news.

No matter how farfetched or how discouraging the talk, the
young priest followed it with avidity. Years later he said, "I noticed that the side that is winning tends to give accurate reports.
The losing side distorts. When the Americans were losing, early
in the war, their news releases were all out of touch with the real
situation, but the Japanese were fairly accurate. The Americans
became more reliable as victory neared. By then the Japanese were
distorting the truth far more than the Americans had. A Japanese
propaganda officer reported that the United States mainland had
been bombed several times by Imperial Nipponese planes and 'the
Yanks, at present, are living a melancholy life.' "

One of Colonel Fertig's men developed a radio of sorts, a Rube
Goldberg device that somehow worked. Day after day the signal

officer tapped out a one-sentence message that he hoped would make contact with an American station and attract a reply. He thought that the sentence, "We have the hot dope on the hot Yanks in the hot Philippines," sounded very American. At the receiving end in San Francisco everybody agreed that it had the faked sound of a Japanese message and so refused to answer.

Father Cronin became friends with another American officer, Captain Charles Smith. After the missionary's parishioners had found one of Smith's friends lost in the hills, the captain came to the *convento* to say thanks. Colonel Fertig was there at the time. Smith announced that he and Captain A.Y. Smith and Captain Jordan Hamner hoped to sail to Australia in a small native-built craft. He promised that upon arrival he would make a plea at MacArthur's headquarters for aid to the Philippines.

"Charley, have you ever done any sailing?" asked Fertig.

"No, Wendell, but I figure I'll sure as hell learn on the way."

Father Cronin's cook, listening to the conversation on the verandah, volunteered for the trip. Since the cook was better at listening than at preparing food, the missionary felt no deep sense of loss.

The cook and the three Americans were not far out when it became evident that the craft was too fragile for the long sea voyage. They returned hurriedly to the remote bay from which they had sailed. By now the cook had seen enough of the open sea and gladly returned to Father Cronin's kitchen.

The Americans were still determined to get to Australia. With money borrowed from Father Cronin and a few other people they went south to Bonifacio to buy a 26-foot craft with a defective Japanese diesel engine.

Father Cronin wrote later: "After much preparation and many delays due to engine trouble and lack of fuel and oil, they were ready to sail in December, 1942. They invited me to go along, but I felt I should stay with my people.

"In this small boat with only a mining compass and a National Geographic map of the southwest Pacific, which I gave them, they sailed for Australia. Before they left, I also gave them a small edition of the New Testament.

"For twenty-five days they sailed down through the seas of the southwest Pacific, calling in at the smaller islands, where they were likely to meet no Japanese, to replenish their water and food supply. Just north of New Guinea they were chased by a Japanese launch but managed to escape."

The crew sailed 1,400 miles across water patrolled by enemy destroyers, corvettes, and launches. Even though the Japanese had landed at Borneo, the Celebes, Sumatra, Java, and other islands between Mindanao and Australia, the little boat slipped through.

Archbishop Cronin still recalls the dramatic stories the Americans told him: "One night when the water was rough, a large swell hit their boat and capsized it, throwing two of the men into the water and imprisoning Captain Smith in the engine room. For a moment all seemed lost, but suddenly the boat righted itself. These engineers had so placed the engine and loaded the boat that it was perfectly balanced, and the next wave caught the overturned boat and spun it right side up, saving the men from watery graves.

"For two and a half days they sailed without food, and drank only such rain water as they could accumulate from the squalls. Suddenly out of the sea appeared a lighthouse and land. They were observed, and ten minutes later, a plane was circling low over them in an unfriendly manner. One of the Moro seamen jumped into the sea with fright, but they fished him out. Soon an army launch approached and brought them to the lighthouse, which proved to be just twenty-five miles north of Darwin. What a marvelous piece of navigation with such scanty equipment."

In a few months a submarine, 325 feet long, surfaced south of Bonifacio. Captain Smith hurried from the submarine to find Father Cronin, saying, "I came to pay back what I owe you. And by the way here is some Mass wine." He said that four tons of equipment were on board—radios, carbines, and ammunition.

Salt and sugar also arrived to add some zest to a bland diet. Most important were atabrine for malaria and several medicines that helped cure dysentery. A few luxuries came, too. Among them were chocolate bars with wrappers displaying crossed American and Filipino flags and the message: I Shall Return— MacArthur.

While the submarine was bringing things good for the morale it also brought some news hard to accept—the realization that "the aid" would not be coming for a long time. Before the arrival of the submarine everyone spoke of "the aid," meaning American troops storming ashore to drive the Japanese from Mindanao once and for all.

Now they heard that when MacArthur arrived in Australia he had learned that the Philippines were near the bottom of the list in the big strategic scheme of things. The Germans were overrunning Europe, chasing the Russians eastward, and doing well in North Africa, too. The Japanese had things all their way in China and in Burma, and they threatened India. The barefoot Filipino fighters could consider themselves expendable.

Before Captain Charles Smith had sailed for Australia, Fertig gave him a radio signal known only to the two of them: MSF—meaning Mindanao Smith Fertig. After reaching Australia the San Francisco station was told to send the prearranged signal. Father Cronin was standing at the wireless on that dark and rainy night, February 2, 1943, when the signal came through. The following day contact was established with Washington and later with General MacArthur's headquarters in Australia.

By establishing this contact with the outside world, Fertig confirmed his standing as The One. This was reinforced when a radio message came through awarding him the Distinguished Service Cross. The message was from MacArthur and bore the congratulations of President Manuel Quezon.

Now wherever Fertig went the Filipinos greeted him in a way that made his itinerary something of a movable feast. Father Cronin's former parishioners in Tangub welcomed the guerrilla leader with such affection that it brought tears to his eyes. Fishermen and their families, dressed in their *fiesta* best, held aloft coconut-oil lamps to light the way for the native outrigger to bring Fertig to their shore. Accompanied by three guitars, an accordion, and a violin, they sang, "Somm-whaare ovvaa de rain-bow. . . ."

On the submarine from Australia came a stocky man, Lieutenant Commander Charles Parsons. He arrived as MacArthur's special agent disguised with a pseudonym and a thick beard. No sooner had he stepped ashore, however, than an old laundry woman cried, "Señor Chick!" She remembered him from his days in Zamboanga before the war.

Chick Parsons had been coowner of the Luzon Stevedoring Corporation. When the Japanese invaded Luzon, he had been repatriated as the Panamanian consul. Although an American citizen he was not flying under false colors, because before the war it was the custom of small nations to appoint consuls from among businessmen in Manila. No sooner did Parsons reach the States than he volunteered for the navy. Because of his background, MacArthur borrowed him and nine months later he was back on Philippine soil.

Archbishop Cronin recalls that Parsons brought Fertig a message from MacArthur concerning the new role the guerrillas must play: quit trying to kill Japanese; gather information instead. Parsons told Fertig: "What MacArthur wants is information. Not twenty Japs dead in some gulch. The radios we brought you are for information. You are to establish a flash line of watching stations along the coast, and pass the word to us of Jap ship movements. We will have subs waiting for these ships. One torpedo in half a second can blow up more ammunition than the Japs would shoot at you in a year. Another can kill more Japs on a troop ship than all the guerrillas on the Islands could ever kill."

So Fertig ordered his guerrillas to surround and protect strategic observation stations on every coast. Transmitters came in by submarine and some were built. The Filipinos kept batteries charged with water wheels, cornmills, foot chargers, and auto chargers.

The system worked. For example, one day in May, 1943, Fathers Thomas Callanan and Edward Haggerty were passing through a market place set up beside a dusty road when the cry of "Japanese! Japanese!" ran through the crowd. Down the road came an armed guard with a dozen prisoners. The captive Japanese officer, who spoke English well, told the priests that two Japanese ships had been sunk.

Scarcely a week went by without someone witnessing a sinking off the coast of Mindanao. When that happened the news raced through the *barrios,* up into the jungles, and across the mountains.

Those thousands of eyes on the hills reported all movements of enemy ships and flights of planes. From these bits and pieces American Intelligence officers learned where enemy power formed and the direction in which it moved. With the help of the Mindanao network the enemy fleet was destroyed by the United States Navy off the Marianas.

From three tons of equipment the submarine tonnage increased until eventually the largest sub in the world, the *USS Narwhal* brought in ninety tons of supplies. On the return trip to Australia the submarines carried civilians from Mindanao. Time and again the Columban Fathers and Sisters had a chance to leave but preferred to stay. Knowing this the Filipinos developed an affection for them that carried over into peacetime.

Besides gathering information, Fertig's guerrillas kept 150,000 Japanese from feeling free to go to other islands in the South Pacific where serious fighting was in progress. In time, General Morimoto, the Japanese commander, decided to put an end to Fertig's annoyances. He planned Operation Big Voice with the mission of silencing Fertig's radios, utterly destroying the guerrilla movement, and killing Fertig. Double agents reported all of this to the guerrilla headquarters.

12 ✛ Close Calls

The more the Japanese increased their activity the harder it was for the missionaries to go about their work. As Father Edward Haggerty wrote in his book, *Guerrilla Padre:* "We saw hundreds of thousands now without the sacraments. Father Cronin obtained leave to go to Cotabato, but both Colonel Bowler and I persuaded him the journey was too hazardous and might simply lose us another priest who was badly needed in his own parish."

Even in his own parish Father Cronin was having close calls. On one occasion, when he hid in a cornfield with some of his parishioners, an old lady made the mistake of bringing her *carabao* with her. The beast made so much noise chomping the corn that it nearly attracted the attention of the Japanese.

One night, when Father Cronin slept in a house half hidden by dwarf coconut trees, the Japanese entered several houses less than a hundred yards away. Perhaps his was missed because it was dark while the others, because of the children in them, kept coconut oil burning through the night.

Thirty-five years later the archbishop described another close call. "I looked down the hill and saw a Japanese patrol walking along the valley road in the direction I wanted to go to visit one of our priests. So I followed well behind them on horseback. Things went well until my return trip when I met a young Filipino and we went along the road together. Suddenly he stopped and said he was turning back. He saw the tips of three rifles sticking above the tall grass a few yards ahead.

"I didn't see them. My eyes haven't been too good since seminary days. But I had no time to doubt the accuracy of his observation. A rifle cracked. Something like a buzzing bee went past.

"I kicked my heels into the horse's side. A sitting target. At full gallop I jumped off and rolled into the tall grass. The density of the underbrush was such that I had to get down on hands and knees to penetrate it. Exhausted, I rolled into a hole, only to find it filled with black ants.

"My glasses were missing. The only pair I owned. I couldn't bear to think of going through the war without glasses so I crawled back, and there they were in the center of the road. Inch by inch I eased out to regain them.

"How to regain the horse? Especially the saddle. I climbed a tree to get direction. After fording a river I came to a *barrio* that had caught the runaway. They heard the shot and when the riderless horse came galloping down the road they recognized it and began to cry, 'The padre is dead! The padre is dead!' The news raced through the hills. Wherever I went for weeks I had to explain that I was still alive. By the way, the Japanese captured the horse and saddle."

The next adventure came at sea when Father Cronin was crossing Panguil Bay traveling from Bonifacio to Baray. He was carrying a sack of rice to Father Merlin Thibault, a Jesuit who dearly needed the food because the great locust plague had left him near starvation.

The small outrigger could not sail during the day because of a lack of breeze, and besides the Japanese might intercept it. At midnight a breeze came up and Father Cronin and two companions set sail. The breeze grew and grew in velocity until waves threatened to sink the boat.

An empty salmon can was the only thing available for bailing water. Slowly the boat submerged until it was a foot below the surface, with only the outrigger keeping things afloat. When the three men drifted ashore at nine in the morning they found the rice was ruined.

"So our well-meant effort," said the archbishop thirty-five years later, "resulted in the Jesuit having to feed three more mouths during a two-day visit."

The Columban sisters experienced their share of such close calls. Four of them in Misamis felt the jolt of war one Sunday during Mass. Just as the bell rang for the elevation a bombardment shook the church. Father Gerald Byrne continued with the Mass and the sisters remained calm.

As Mother Francis DeSales said later, "We knew what it was.

There was no need to go out and look. Three Japanese destroyers had come into the bay and were shelling Misamis. It was the signal for the total abandonment of the town. We left as soon as the Mass was finished, and with the rest of the town, headed for the hills.

"In three years we made ten moves. The Japanese let it be known that they would punish anyone who had escaped. That meant us. We had to be careful. One midnight, word came that the Japanese were near. We fled to the home of friends on the shore of Misamis Bay. The house was built on stilts, and the crocodile-infested water could be seen through the floor."

Since they did not want to endanger the lives of their friends, the sisters asked the man of the house to take them out along the bay to look for a safer spot. In the boat they stretched out beneath a covering of banana leaves to run the gauntlet of searching Japanese eyes. The sisters took nothing with them except two books for spiritual reading—the New Testament and Father De-Jaegher's *The Virtue of Trust*.

After several hours the boat reached a branch in a river. Which way to go? The sisters decided in favor of the stream on the right.

"It was a providential decision," said Mother Francis De Sales, "for soon an island appeared in the distance. As we pulled up on the shore a native came running down from the hills. We greeted him and asked the name of the island. He gave a word in dialect, *"Sumalig,"* which means trust. I glanced at the book in my hand, *The Virtue of Trust.*"

13 ✤ Martyrs in Manila

Close shaves were all part of a day's work as far as the American guerrillas were concerned. They used to tell of them while sitting on Father Cronin's verandah smoking cigarettes carelessly rolled with old magazines, toilet tissue, love letters, or bamboo skin.

They often wondered how things were going on the island of Luzon, especially around Manila. Was it rougher up there? At such times Father Cronin thought of his American classmate, Father Vincent McFadden, a prisoner of war.

Father McFadden had been moved from the camp at Davao on Mindanao to the University of Santo Tomas, a camp for civilians in the heart of Manila. There, while serving as a hospital orderly with five other priests and a miner from South Africa, he witnessed the destructive effect of anxiety, beriberi, dysentery, and general debility. He came to admire the hospital director, Dr. Stevenson, a Protestant medical missionary, who enraged the Japanese by insisting on writing "malnutrition" on many death certificates. The Japanese suggested he change this to "heart failure" and when the doctor refused they put him in solitary confinement.

The first Columban to die in the war was Father Francis Douglas. His first parish in the Philippines, in the town of Pillila, had a church that was falling apart, a rectory that resembled an abandoned factory, and a population of Aglipayans and neglected Catholics.

Before he could begin to make headway the Japanese invaded the islands. During the occupation he kept to his post for two years. His parishioners said that the Japanese finally arrested him because Filipino guerrillas were sneaking in from the hills to go to confession.

For three days Father Douglas stood tied to a pillar in the rear of the church while being tortured, starved, and threatened. His face was bloody, one eye was black and swollen, his arms were severely bruised.

Even his captors were impressed with his calm. A Japanese officer told one of the parishioners, "I admire the man. He knows how to suffer. He's been there three days and nights but shows no sign of impatience."

How or when death came is not certain. One day in 1943 several Japanese soldiers led the priest away and no one has seen or heard of Father Douglas since.

The greatest horror of the war came on February 3, 1945, when shelling began and lasted for most of the month. The Americans had landed on Leyte in October and were now fighting the Japanese for possession of Manila. In the district called Malate, the Columban school, used as a hospital for three years, was caught in the crossfire, and so was the lovely Spanish church. At least 500 parishioners died in the siege. Every priest in the parish was killed.

Father McFadden wrote to his Columban superiors: "On Tuesday, February 13th, Father John Lalor together with a Dr. Antonio Lahorra and several of the workers went into their air-raid shelter for a few hours' rest. They had had a particularly busy time in the operating room and were completely exhausted. Shortly after they entered the shelter, a shell crashed into the building just above their heads and all inside were killed instantly—mercifully, as it happened, since the shelter burned furiously. The zone was then, and still is, a combat zone, and nothing could be done about burying the bodies. I was allowed to go down there on the 18th and discovered his body, which the nurse helped me identify. We buried him in the school yard, with bullets flying all around."

In that school yard the children used to greet the Columbans in a chorus of treble voices: "Gud ap-ter-noon Fadder. God bless you."

The priests answered slowly and distinctly, for the children spoke Tagalog at home: "Good af-ter-noon, chil-dren. God bless you!"

The deaths of four other Columbans in Malate are still a mystery. Fathers John Heneghan, Patrick Kelly, Peter Fallon, and Joseph Monaghan were taken captive early in the siege. The surviving parishioners say that the priests and many of the menfolk of the parish were taken from the church and headed toward Pasay. They were never seen again. The prevailing rumor is that they were tortured, covered with gasoline, and burned.

Now that the war with all of its dangers and hardships is long past, what Archbishop Cronin best remembers is the generosity of the people. In the presence of such hospitality, he and the other Columbans and the American guerrilla fighters felt humble. Those men in hiding never worried about getting help but they did feel concern in trying to keep the people from doing too much.

As Father Haggerty wrote in his journal: "You may eat at any house as a matter of course, and the owners are ashamed if they cannot borrow plates and a table cloth, rice and sugar for you. People will give you the only bed, or having none, the best mat and pillows. They will serve you their last chicken, eggs, and rice and silently go hungry themselves."

One of the best explanations of why the missionaries on Mindano survived the war so well was given years later by Father Callanan. "The war came along at just the right time for us. We had been here a couple of years, long enough to get the lay of the land. And we were young! Yes, the big thing was we were young. If that happened now, we'd never survive it!"

14 ✢ Appointment to Zamboanga

A fter the war Father Cronin remained in Bonifacio for a short time before being transferred to Aurora in the province of Zamboanga. In 1950 he was asked to start a parish in remote Salug, also in Zamboanga.

Salug had a reputation of being about the most difficult·assignment in Mindanao. The Malingdang Mountains and the Midsalip ranges are rugged; the Salug, Mahayag and Guitran rivers have a habit of flooding. All manner of insect life thrives in a country that seems to be either dense with forests or deep in mud. The parish is strung out across vast distances with dozens of *barrios* reached by slippery mountain trails where two steps forward are followed by one slip backward.

The name of Salug was eventually changed to Molave, but as Salug it had developed a notoriety that had reached as far away as the seminary where the mention of the name brought a certain awe. So when a young priest, Father James Mulroy, who had not heard about the change of name, was told he would be a curate in Molave, he sighed, "Thank God it's not Salug!"

Molave was one of the homesteading towns encouraged by President Manuel Quezon when he promoted the opening of Mindanao's interior shortly before the war. The town, in the heart of homesteading activity, was named after the molave tree which has lumber so tough it defies the sharp-toothed termite, so strong it supports heavy loads, and so heavy that it sinks in water. President Quezon said he wished to make the Filipino nation "as strong as the molave."

The citizens of Molave are as tough and sturdy as the trees. With nothing more than the family water buffalo they crossed rivers, penetrated the uplands, and cleared land to plant rice and corn. Not having axes and horses they could not hack down and haul away primeval trees and so they burned them and left blackened stumps to rot away with time. The farmers plowed around the stumps. When the foliage no longer blocked the sun, a harvest of sorts developed.

Every village in the hills built its own chapel. These were usually tiny buildings of bamboo and palm leaves. Since Father Cronin wanted to visit most villages once a month he spent much of the time in the saddle.

Sometimes not even a horse could reach a village. In speaking of one such place, Father Cronin used to tell the newly arrived young priests, "Don't say you have been on the missions until you have seen Midsalip."

Midsalip is twenty-five miles from the nearest road. When Father Cronin left the road and headed into the forest it meant a day of hiking and climbing to an extensive plateau about two thousand feet above sea level. Only a local guide could find the trail that lead through thick woods and heavy undergrowth, a way blocked with fallen trees that meandered up and down endless hills.

The founder of Midsalip, Candido Alhas, is one of the most interesting men Patrick Cronin has ever met. Candido came from the island of Siquigur, where as a small boy he was so seriously ill he almost died. His mother, despairing of all human help, made a solemn promise to spread devotion to St. Joseph if he recovered.

Candido recovered, and after his mother's death took it upon himself to carry out her promise. He decided that the best way to spread devotion to St. Joseph was to have him named patron of some village. But every village in his native island already had a patron. Eventually he emigrated to Mindanao in search of new land. Here, too, he found that every little village had a patron.

When the war came, Candido did what so many others in the Philippines did, he left his home to flee to the mountains. During this time he met a tribe of pagans called Subanos who told him of the fertile plateau of Midsalip. They described the virgin forest as yet uninhabited except for some of their tribe.

In November of 1945 Candido visited Midsalip with a party of Subanos as guides. After three days of hard going through thick forests he reached the plateau. It was a land of promise. He also saw a chance of fulfilling his mother's promise. He explored the area and then returned to his home.

The following March he and his wife and family set out for

Midsalip. Up and down the rugged mountains they carried a prized possession, a statue of St. Joseph. With the help of the Subanos, Candido built a small chapel and installed the statue.

Three years later, in 1949, Candido saw the culmination of his hopes when Father Cronin made the grueling trip to Midsalip for the first time. On March 19, the feast of St. Joseph, he dedicated the chapel and community to their patron and celebrated the first Mass ever said in the new settlement.

Through the years, Molave and the territory around it continued to be a rough assignment. Twenty years after Father Cronin's first visit, Father Eamon Fleming wrote: "A priest in the newly developing areas is a man in the saddle a good part of the time. While the average parish has a jeep, with four-wheel drive for the hills, there are many places around Molave where even a jeep cannot go. We then saddle the parish horse and take off with our Mass kit through the hills, often crossing waist-deep streams of swiftly flowing water and hacking our way through jungle growth.

"I recall more than one occasion on which I had no horse and had to ride a buffalo bareback, a thing which comes easy to the supple-bodied Filipino but not quite so easy to the foreigner. Then one time I put a western saddle on the back of a buffalo. It was hardly successful as the contours of a water buffalo are not made for a western saddle."

Through the years the conveniences of life around Molave have improved, but not much. Things began looking up in 1958 when the White Eagle Company, which mines copper, cut a dirt road through the rugged country so that what used to be a one-day walk now became a one-hour bus ride. Admittedly, the quality of the bus ride was such that the passenger often wished he had walked.

Father Gabriel Koehane said, "It's still a nice parish if you like to walk." He walks a great deal except when he gets up enough courage to ride the bus. It frightens him at some of the river crossings when the fan belt is removed and the conductor sits on the hood to become the navigator of a bus plowing through water up to its headlights. Often the vehicle gets stuck and unless another bus comes along real soon it begins to sink into the sand.

When the water comes through the windows the passengers start swimming for their lives.

"There's a good-natured rivalry among the bus drivers," said Father Keohane. "They taunt one another about who will cross first. Passengers and spectators offer lots of advice and encouragement. But sometimes the water is too high for the bus to cross. So passengers transfer to horseback, or to a *carabao,* a powerful swimmer. That's an awkward ride because all of the hide moves. The best bet that I've found is to grasp the beast's tail with one hand and with the other grasp the beast's owner who rides up front."

Although Father Cronin felt the severity of life in Zamboanga right after the war, he knew that on all the islands conditions were difficult. In December of 1945 Father Richard Grimme arrived in Mindanao and reported back to the states: "Things are as scarce down here as they are in Manila—perhaps even more so. Vestments, religious articles, books, and clothing are needed most. What vestments we have are in a dilapidated condition and the wine for Mass is still being measured with a medicine dropper.

"Food is scarce and rough and is mostly of the tinned variety, rice and meat being luxuries priced far beyond the capacity of our purse. The priests have managed to clothe themselves, albeit in haphazard fashion, and most of them have succeeded in preserving some old relic of a soutane for festive wear. I had occasion, however, to practice the precept of the Gospel and bestow one of my two soutanes on Father Joe Grimley, who had none.

"In spite of this scarcity of even the necessaries, the priests are well and happy. For myself, I am filled with that contentment that a man feels when he has reached the place that he knows is his own place, and sees before him the work that he has to do."

Father Cronin understood what Father Grimme meant by the contentment that comes when a man reaches the place he knows is his own place and sees before him the work that he has to do. And yet he could never escape the question, "Why me?" Why should someone born in Moneygall and reared in Tullamore dedicate his life to a place like Zamboanga?

15 ✢ Life Speeds Up

Although Patrick Cronin was in the remote province of Zamboanga in the years following the war, he still sensed the beat of life increasing in Mindanao. The faster tempo showed up in transportation more than in any other way. The horse was on his way to becoming an anachronism when bulldozers began cutting roads through ancient trails, and bridges were built across rivers forded for centuries.

The bridges, often constructed first, were kept in better condition than the roads. The reason being that if a road is bad the traveler merely bounces across it, but if a bridge is bad he falls into the river. This led one missionary to observe, "Ah, yes, in the Philippines the roads are good—except for those stretches between the bridges."

The coming of roads and bridges created a world in which it was possible for the parish jeep to operate. The war had introduced the jeep to the South Pacific and scarcely was the last shot fired before the tough little vehicle took its place in missionary work. Less than a decade after the war, a missionary said, "We speak of the contribution to the work of the Church by the arrival of more priests, and by the new communities of sisters, and by the growing numbers of catechists—but what about the parish jeep!"

Speaking in praise of the jeep Father Patrick Hurley said, "Suppose there is an urgent sick call in a *barrio* ten miles away. The priest drops everything, even Sunday Mass, to reach the bedside of a dying Catholic. If there is a parish jeep he can get away at once. If there isn't he may look for transport among his friends in town. That takes up valuable time, and he may look in vain, especially in the season when everybody is out harvesting.

"Walking, except for short distances and outside of the great noonday heat, might be out of the question. I remember two sick calls I made soon after coming to the Philippines, and each taught me a lesson. The first meant only a few miles, but in the noonday heat. I did it on foot and the exertion left me prostrate all that afternoon and the whole next day. The second was a distance of many miles. It was much too far to walk. There was no public transport; I had to wait for about an hour until some neighbors woke up from their *siesta* before I could borrow their jeep. The result? The sick man was dead when I arrived."

Father Hurley said that if a missionary finds that a bus is going in the direction of the sick parishioner, chances are the driver won't leave town until he has enough passengers to pay for the run and that may be for several hours.

Buses, like jeeps, increased after the war and also became legendary. Missionary after missionary added his stories about buses to an evergrowing folklore. An example is Father Stephen Kealy's description of the first he rode in the Philippines: "Suppose you had a new bus, and hired a group of roughnecks armed with sledgehammers, picks, and chisels to do whatever they wished to the bus for about three days, giving the specific instructions to loosen all the screws and break all the glass. All the knobs should be removed from the instruments on the dashboard, and all the wiring connections should be torn loose and left to dangle about the feet of the driver.

"In addition the seats should be sprung from their moorings on the floor, and care should be taken to remove the floor boards over the rear wheels in order that a good sprinkling of mud could splatter the passengers. All painted portions should be disfigured beyond recognition. This is not a pretty picture, but it is no exaggeration."

The archbishop's favorite bus story has as its victim Father Michael Donohue, the Columban superior in the Philippines, who was in Gingoog City visiting Columban pastors in the area. After receiving a call from Manila asking that he return on urgent business, Father Donohue was told that the bus from Gingoog to Cagayan would leave at two in the morning. This suited him fine because then he would be in Cagayan by nine in the morning, with plenty of time to spare before the early afternoon flight to Manila.

The darkness was disturbed at two o'clock when the bus driver honked loud and long outside the *convento,* to awaken every barking dog and crowing rooster in the neighborhood. The

Columban found himself the first passenger. During the next hour the driver stopped at several houses until the passenger list grew to fourteen.

Well along on the journey the driver brought the bus to a sudden halt. After counting the passengers he announced that he was losing money on the trip, and stretched out on the front seat and went to sleep.

As the morning wore on, more and more passengers came aboard. Finally the driver decided the trip was worth his time and energy. It all ended with Father Donohue arriving in Cagayan late in the afternoon, too late for the Manila plane.

Father Michael Cullen said that on one occasion when his bus was about half way to its destination it met a group of people on the road who wished to go in the opposite direction. Since this group was larger than the group on the bus, and since the driver had already collected the fares of those on the bus, he announced that this was the end of the line. He put the passengers off and took in the new group.

Father Cullen will always remember the time a driver, still a considerable distance from his destination, stopped the bus in front of his own house and went to bed for the night. Luckily, on this occasion, one of the passengers knew how to manipulate the loose wires, and he drove the bus into town. But before he reached the bus station he stopped at his own home and also went off to bed smiling graciously at Father Cullen as he alighted.

Sometimes the trip is so hectic that the missionary wishes the driver would stop and go to bed. After a wild ride, a priest pointed to a sign above the driver's head, "God is my copilot" and said, "I doubt that God was consulted about the partnership."

A large highway sign outside of Aurora in Zamboanga reads "God's Country . . . Don't Drive Like Hell!" But most drivers are going too fast to read the sign.

The motorboat joined the jeep and the bus, after the war, as another aid in helping the Columbans carry out their work with more dispatch. The motorboat has also become legendary as folklore accumulated around it like barnacles on a hull.

Take for example the excitement that ran along the coast of Mindanao when Father Patrick Cashman was reported missing, adrift in an open sea without food or water. After visiting Father Thomas Callanan on the mainland he left in a small motorboat for his parish, on the island of Caminguin, for what seemed would be a two-hour trip across a calm moonlit sea.

Father Callanan recalls, "Next afternoon I got a message asking if I knew where he was, as he had not got home. I realized immediately that he must have had engine trouble and was probably adrift at sea. We sent out the alarm and alerted the fishermen over a wide area. We got a well-coordinated search going, and God only knows how many motorboats went out looking for him."

In the town of Catarman, where Father Cashman was pastor, everything came to a standstill. No work of any kind was being done. The people stayed up all night. Every boat in town, and later every boat on the island, took part in the search.

Father Callanan hurried to the island and told the owner of a filling station to supply gasoline to anybody who wanted to join in the search. The Columbans would pay for it. The owner said that he would give the gasoline to anyone who wanted it: "After all, do you think you priests are the only ones who care about Father Cashman?"

Finally after drifting for two days and two nights the priest was picked up. He was in an uncovered boat without food or water and it was midsummer. Although he came through the experience in good condition, everyone agreed he could not have taken much more of that tropical sun. One of the first things Father Cashman said to his rescuers was, "Thank God for the old-fashioned rosary!"

Although the Columbans own no airplanes, they sometimes use commercial flights to save time and energy. The five-hundred-mile trip by boat from Manila to Mindanao, so time-consuming and wearing, can now be made by Philippine Airlines in one hour and twenty minutes. Small commercial planes are time-savers in their connecting flights between the main towns on the island; for example, the trip from Cagayan de Oro to Ozamis City takes most of the day by bus and boat but can be made in a twenty-minute flight in a small plane.

Such improvements in transportation were of great help to

Patrick Cronin when he was appointed apostolic administrator of the prelature of Ozamis. Suddenly, he was in a position that required him to visit priests scattered over a large area of western Mindanao. Time and energy seemed more precious than ever and he realized his hiking and horseback days were just about over.

16 ✣ Realizing a Need

At age thirty-eight Patrick Cronin became a monsignor. Archbishop James T. Hayes, S.J., of Cagayan, installed him as apostolic administrator of the new Diocese of Ozamis on May 20, 1952. The title of apostolic administrator meant that the monsignor would be performing all functions of a bishop, except that of ordaining priests.

Two thousand parishioners packed the wood-and-concrete cathedral in Ozamis City to attend the installation. Ninety priests crowded the sanctuary.

In his sermon that day, Archbishop Hayes recalled that the Columbans had increased their number of priests in the area from the original ten in 1938 to forty in 1952, and their parishes from nine to twenty. Where there had been but one Catholic high school there were now fifteen, plus three colleges; the largest, with 1,200 students, was conducted by Columban sisters in Ozamis City. This growth was remarkable, observed Archbishop Hayes, since it happened in only thirteen years, four of which were filled with war.

Archbishop Hayes described the new prelature as comprising the provinces of Misamis Occidental and Lanao, both formerly a part of his Archdiocese of Cagayan. He said that the prelature numbered 300,000 Catholics and 320,000 non-Catholics, some of whom were schismatic, some Protestant, but most Muslim.

Monsignor Cronin heard these statistics with awe. In retrospect, life seemed simple in Bonifacio, Aurora, and Molave. All of this was so complicated. Soon he would learn that each day brings events that lead to a clearer realization of what is really needed, and so one gradually grows from neophyte to old hand.

One such day of realization came four months later, on the feast of St. Michael, September 29. The monsignor was in the port city of Iligan, a great Catholic center since Spanish times, even though located in the province of Lanao, the stronghold of Islam on Mindanao. He had come down from Ozamis City for the *fiesta,* which is celebrated with an exuberance introduced by Spanish missionaries.

Roads and trails were crowded with thousands of people coming to church for Mass, which was offered every half hour from five until nine in the morning. Throughout the Masses the statue of St. Michael sat in a great chariot near the high altar with innumerable votive candles burning before it.

The chariot with the statue was drawn through the streets in procession during the afternoon. Noise filled the air as the martial music of two bands and the racket from guns, revolvers, and firecrackers did honor to the warrior angel. Men and women, dressed as angels and devils, fought mock battles in front of the chariot. The thud-thud of wooden swords striking wooden shields could be heard above the din, as combatants recalled a war waged long ago. The devils yielded obligingly to the angels as St. Michael reentered the church. The pandemonium of battle was followed by the serene strains of *O Salutaris* and the service of Benediction spread a calm over the end of the day.

Crowds gathered in the church the following morning with candidates for confirmation ranging in age from children just baptized to old people not long for this world. For four days the monsignor was kept busy administering the sacrament to some 3,000 people.

He recalled later, "My work in Iligan done, I proceeded to the outlying villages. Father Brangan, Iligan's pastor, had mapped out my program—there were seven villages and I was to take four on the first day and three on the second. The work in the first three proved less arduous than I had anticipated, the numbers for confirmation totaled scarcely more than 500. When we reached the fourth village in midafternoon one look at the crowd made it clear that here was a very different matter and that a busy evening stretched ahead."

The monsignor edged his way to the village chapel which was about thirty feet wide and sixty long. As he entered, the crowd surged in after him until he guessed there must have been nearly a thousand people in a space so confining that the frail timber walls seemed ready to burst. The press of bodies was such that the doors had to be closed, leaving outside many who clamored for admission. Within, the heat was intense and movement well nigh impossible.

Parents tried to push their children toward Monsignor Cronin and shouted to attract his attention. Sponsors were unable to get near the children. The monsignor and his assistants, Fathers Brangan, Ruddy, and Gaffney, were sweating until their soutanes hung limp from head to foot.

"Suddenly I grew afraid," recalled Patrick Cronin. "It needed only someone to faint, some slight accident among that tightly packed crowd and we should easily have had a panic. Possibly resulting in the death of many. I ordered the doors to be opened, then proceeded through the church and into the open plaza, confirming as I went. The people followed me and the rest of the ceremony was held in the open air. For what seemed an age I went on administering the sacrament until darkness fell at six o'clock. Even then there were still many to be attended to and it was not until nearly seven that I was finished."

That evening Monsignor Cronin counted the certificates and found that he had confirmed 783 people that afternoon. After visiting the remaining three villages the following day the total number of confirmations for the week was near 5,000.

As he and Father William Adams drove back to Iligan that night they felt the full burden of all of those statistics. What they had seen in recent days had made them more aware than ever of the need for more priests. This need became a recurring theme in Patrick Cronin's awareness from that day on.

Three years later, September 25, 1955, the monsignor became a bishop and used the occasion of his consecration to speak of the lack of priests in the Philippines. He addressed his words to the many prelates who gathered for the ceremony at St. Columban's College, at Navan, in Ireland.

Soon after Bishop Cronin had returned to Mindanao he began writing articles for the three Columban magazines published in Ireland, Australia, and the United States, telling the story in as many dramatic ways as he could: "Several parishes with four to seven priests in pastoral work are listed in the Philippine Catholic Directory as having populations of 62,000, 73,000, 87,000, 90,000, and even 120,000! I doubt if similar figures can be found in any other part of the Catholic world."

Since then the growth of a native-born clergy has provided Patrick Cronin with a few brighter statistics. About the time he became Archbishop of Cagayan de Oro, in 1970, he wrote: "Many new seminaries have developed in the Philippines since the war. Now in the 14 major seminaries there are 1,012 students and the 31 minor seminaries cater to 3,147 students."

Although the Philippines are still short of priests, the Filipino clergy are beginning to become missionaries themselves. This is in accordance with a wish expressed by the assembled prelates at Vatican II: "It is very fitting that the young churches should participate as soon as possible in the universal missionary work of the Church. Let them send their own missionaries to proclaim the gospel all over the world, even though they themselves are suffering from a shortage of clergy."

17 ✢ Thanks to the Laymen

Archbishop Cronin makes the point that even in Spanish times the ratio of priests to parishioners was better than it is now. At the end of the last century 3,500 priests cared for 5 million Catholics; now 5,000 priests care for 33 million Catholics. Fortunately, there is a tradition of an active lay apostolate in the Philippines, one that began with the Spanish padres.

Even one dedicated layman in a village can make the difference between a practially dead faith and a lively spiritual life. One such, Meling Nemeno, lived in the village of Mansanas when Patrick Cronin was pastor of Molave. After the war Meling married a Cebu girl and the couple left Ozamis City to search out the great tracts of land being opened in the province of Zamboanga. They paused briefly at Molave before pushing into the wilderness that rises toward the Malindang mountains.

A trading center developed where Meling settled. One of the young Filipino's first acts was to build a small chapel and invite the priest from Molave to say Mass in honor of the village's patron, St. Vincent Ferrer. To make monthly visits the Columban had to cover twenty miles each way on horseback, with the horse slipping and stumbling over mud-covered rocks much of the way.

What a relief it was when, arriving tired and wet after four hours in the saddle, we saw the welcome lights of a small village across the river. The horse splashed through the swollen stream and clambered up the opposite bank. Almost immediately a light appeared on the verandah of the largest house in the village and a cheery voice called out, *"Maayong Gabii, Padre."* (Good evening, Father.) Handsome Meling and his charming wife seated the missionary in a small room behind the chapel, just as their two older children arrived with bowls of steaming rice, chicken, and eggs.

A decade after Patrick Cronin's last visit to the trading center, another Columban was still making the trip. He said, "The ride is long and tiresome. Often in the rainy season I arrive soaked to the skin. But I am always certain of a hearty welcome. There will be many for confession and communion. The people will listen carefully to my sermon or instruction, and there will never be even a smile, and certainly not a sneer, at my midwest American pronunciation of the local dialect. After the Mass there are plenty of babies to baptize and maybe a sick call. It is a pleasant and inspiring place to be and often I wish I could spend more than just one day a month at Mansanes. Thanks to Meling Nemeno, and others like him, villages like Mansanes are not rare in the Philippines."

Sometimes one Meling working alone isn't enough. A large group of well-trained laymen might be needed at once. Whenever this need arises the required number somehow seems to be there. Sister Maureen Kearns, a Columban nun, told of such an occasion:

"It was a big thing when the principal of the public high school allowed us to visit the campus an hour each week. But there were 2,000 students! That meant providing forty-four catechists if we were to meet all the students in every section.

"Where to get all those catechists! The answer lay in our college students. More than enough volunteered to do in-service training so that they could help teach religion in the public school."

Each week Sister Maureen, two lay teachers, and Fathers Patrick O'Donovan and Hans Meyer met to draw up an outline of the lesson plan. Each catechist was given a copy, and on Saturday morning all met for a demonstration of the prepared lesson in the native dialect and in English.

"This Saturday class for catechists is the key to the effectiveness of the whole system," said Sister Maureen. "After the class each catechist draws up a lesson plan to fit the age and background of those to be taught.

"The college students are aware of the spiritual responsibility entailed in their catechetical work. They realize it's not just knowledge they are imparting. They are imparting themselves."

Some of the lay workers are difficult to classify. What name could be given to the dozen unmarried women who work so hard in the rural parish of Lopez-Jaena? They are "angels" to Father

Malachy Toner, who is expected to reach 17,000 parishioners scattered over a vast area.

In describing his plight, the middle-aged Columban said, "An asphalt road skirts the coast for six miles or so. From it into the hills run what are euphemistically called 'feeder roads'—but when it rains that is another story. There are no telephones, of course, and no regular transportation. And naturally I have no assistant priest, no brothers, no nuns.

"These twelve women are more than catechists. They are not nuns, and don't want to be. Yet their neighbors do call them *madrecitas,* 'little sister,' the Spanish term for nun. They are prepared to dedicate their lives, in part, to serve the needs of the Church. All teach catechism and do census work. All visit the aged and the poor. All of them prepare young couples for the sacrament of matrimony."

Some have specialities, too. Benita Montefalcon runs a nutrition program for malnourished children in three villages. Basilin Camingoa takes care of the vestments and linens and leads the weekly novena. Eduarda Masayon is planning a building project for a *barrio* church. All of them extend the presence of the priest and help make his work more fruitful.

Each First Friday the dozen women meet to plan their activities for the month. Three or four times a year they come together for a few days to deepen their knowledge of their work and their own spiritual life.

"We've had lay missionaries come for a time and then leave," said Father Toner. "They have done fine work. But these women on the spot know the territory, speak the language, live the life, and know the hearts of the people they deal with. They have little to learn, locally speaking. They're part of the scene and they're on it every day.

"In many ways the *madrecitas* are better to have than sisters who are strangers to the locality and usually need transportation from a central convent. With the soaring price of gasoline, that is out of the question. The *madrecitas* are right there when you need them and all the time.

"They can't afford to work for nothing. They come from simple, hard-working families where everyone has to make a personal contribution if the family is to survive. I manage to scrape enough together every month to give them a little something. But the parish is as poor as its people. I'd like to get this pioneering effort on a better footing and give these dedicated workers a feeling of security. Especially since I know, and they know, I'll be transferred in two years in accord with diocesan policy."

Many missionaries feel that a full-time catechist is needed for villages where there are 500 people or more. One Columban said, "In some cases that is the only satisfactory solution. I have in mind two villages where ninety percent of the children have no religion. It is impossible to get volunteer local catechists in such villages because so few have any real instruction in the faith. The answer is to pay a catechist who will go and live there and teach religion in the school as any other subject is taught. Usually that's just a dream because of lack of funds."

A pastor on the coast of Iligan Bay said that the question he hears most is: "Father, why can't we have a catechist?" His answer is always, "I simply haven't the money." And so he goes ahead and trains more volunteer, part-time catechists.

Of all organizations formed by laymen to help the missionary none is more highly regarded than the Legion of Mary. One priest told how groups of eight or more from this organization go to a *barrio* and live there for one or two weeks on a "mission" basis. They begin by visiting every house, often making the first contact ever made. One woman greeted them with, "Come up awhile. You are the first Catholics who have ever visited our home. Only the Jehovah Witnesses ever come here and they give us talks every week."

Next the visitors teach catechism and arrange for baptisms, marriage validations, and sick calls. Toward the end of the group's visit the priest comes to the *barrio* to find everything in readiness. On one such occasion Father John O'Hehir wrote: "For the final two days of the mission I visited the *barrio* and offered my first Mass at the southern end of the area assigned to the mission. Because of the wind and the rain squalls, I expected a very small attendance. To our surprise and consolation, the chapel was filled to overflowing and five *mansebado* couples (living together in common law marriage) came along to be married, and five children were baptized. After Mass I was called to attend two seriously ill adults."

In the Philippines laymen have been effective in developing the *cursillo* movement, a form of spiritual retreat, now called a Christian Community Seminar. A Columban, skeptical of the movement, decided to attend a *cursillo* to see for himself what it was all about.

"I perked up," he said, "when our first lecturer, a layman, launched into his talk. It was about ideals. He told us that only a realist can be a true idealist. There was no oratory for oratory's sake, no striving for effect, no criticism of authority—just straight-from-the-shoulder teaching."

The missionary looked at the fifty-three faces around him—strong, lean faces that one sees on fishing boats, and burned leathery faces from the field. Everyone was listening with intensity.

"What is there about these talks, about this atmosphere, that grips one? There is sincerity, there is conviction, there is interest, there is good delivery—a dozen other compelling features. But no single element, nor all of them put together, can explain the spell fully to me. Could it be the Holy Spirit? Could it be something of the outpouring of grace that charged the words of the apostles and converted 5,000 on the first Pentecost? I'm inclined to think it is."

In the past ten years laymen have been conducting religious services to an extent they never did before. At the start of this new practice a young Columban was startled to see a sign tacked to a chapel door: Priestless Mass Next Sunday.

He said to the sacristan, "Don't you know that the bishop told us not to speak of a 'priestless Mass' but rather a 'priestless service'? You can't have a Mass without a priest." The sacristan explained it was only a slip of the pen.

The missionary hoped he had made it clear to the congregation that the Mass is divided into two parts, the liturgy of the Word of God and the liturgy of sacrifice. He had taken pains to explain, "Only a priest can celebrate the liturgy of sacrifice. You yourselves can celebrate the liturgy of the Word here in your little chapel every Sunday. You're not bound to go to Mass because it's too far away, but you are bound to keep holy the Lord's Day, and what better way than attending this service each Sunday."

At the central church each Sunday, prayer leaders, song leaders, and readers of the epistle, Gospel, and pastor's sermon climb into borrowed jeeps to fan out to remote *barrios*. As a whole the priestless service has been effective, after overcoming a few small problems, one of which was punctuality, not a strong point with the Filipinos. To remedy this the pastor suggested that the services should start at the same time as the Mass in the town so that the people could join in spirit with the priest in the central church. Since then one of the readings begins: "Now the priest is offering the sacrifice in the town. We are sad that we have no priest of our own, but we join our hearts with the sacrifice being offered now by the priest."

The roots of the priestless service go back to December 4, 1963, when the Constitution on the Sacred Liturgy, the first document of the Vatican Council, was published. Article 35 states: "Bible services should be encouraged, especially on the vigils of the more solemn feasts, on some weekdays in Advent and Lent, and on Sundays and feast days. They are particularly to be commended in places where no priest is available."

Archbishop Cronin sees the Columbans as fighting a numbers battle. How to care for so many with so few? Throughout the islands they serve ninety-six parishes and thousands of *barrio* chapels. They are in charge of 117 elementary and secondary schools and 15 colleges with a total enrollment of 60,000 students. And only 233 Columban priests! They realize that they could not possibly carry the burden without the help of thousands and thousands of lay leaders.

18 ✢ Life of the Mind

Hardly had the last shot of the war been fired when General MacArthur urged educators in the Philippines to begin classes "even under the trees." In ruined buildings, Quonset huts, rented rooms, and, yes, even under the trees, the children started classes. In this upsurge of concern for education the Columban priests and sisters shared in the elation of things getting done, of life moving forward.

All of a sudden secondary schools opened in Jimenez, Plaridel, and Tangub, thanks to the vitality of Fathers Thomas Callanan, Francis McCullough, and Olan Healy. In Bonifacio, Patrick Cronin began work on a school, but before it could become a reality he was asked to start a parish in Aurora, in the province of Zamboanga.

His successor, Father John Crafton, brought the school to completion. The new pastor at Bonifacio was one of the young Americans who had arrived shortly after the war to relieve the pioneering band, all of whom needed rest and medical treatment at home. These young priests proceeded to expand the existing schools and to open new ones.

Their zest and ingenuity overcame the lack of buildings, staff, and money. In many cases the priest screened off a corner of his *convento* for living quarters and remodeled the rest for use as a school. Additional rooms were built of bamboo and *sawali* leaves.

Teaching sisters made the exciting growth possible. The Franciscan Missionaries of Mary, the Congregation of Religious of the Virgin Mary, and the Sisters of St. Columban had been in Mindanao before the war and now returned to their schools to renew their work. They were soon joined by the Sisters of Mercy, St. Paul de Chartres, and Maryknolls.

In describing the success of some of these women, Patrick Cronin wrote: "It is with a certain hesitation that I speak of the work of the Sisters of St. Columban in Ozamis City. I have watched their progress since their arrival here in 1940, and while it is true that only one who has been a witness to the work can properly appreciate the magnitude of it, still no words of mine are adequate to describe that achievement. It is the story of a success attained after a long struggle against overwhelming odds."

When the Columban Sisters arrived in Mindanao in 1940 they found elementary classes being taught in a poorly equipped small building. Scarcely had they developed a better school than the island was invaded and the Japanese took over their buildings. For the next four years the sisters lived in the mountains, hiding like fugitives.

Upon returning to Ozamis City they faced a discouraging situation. Only the frame of their school remained. The Japanese had torn down the walls for firewood. Desks, blackboards, and library were also gone. The sisters began rebuilding immediately and within a year added a College of Liberal Arts and Education.

"They faced immense difficulties," recalls the archbishop, "especially after the ravages of war. In 1948 they built an entirely new school and each year the size of the student body grows and the number of courses offered increases."

Years later one of the Columban Sisters in Ozamis, Sister Mary Sheila, recalled the satisfaction that came during that period of rapid growth. "Years ago a friend of mine advised, 'Don't ever be a teacher! If you are, your life won't be worth living.' I know now that was a superficial remark. I thank God he saw fit to send me to the Philippines as a teacher."

Sister Mary Sheila found Filipino children delightfully simple. "They love stories, especially those from the Gospels. When I told them the story of the prodigal son they listened entranced. The following day I asked for volunteers to retell the story. There was a surging forest of hands. Little Lourdes in the front row, the smallest in the class, was literally jumping out of her seat with eagerness. I took pity on her. 'There was a rich man once,' she began, gasping with excitement, 'who had two sons.' Then the rest of the story came tumbling out. Suddenly I heard, 'The other son went to a foreign country and there spent all his money, having a good time with his girl friend.' "

Sister Mary Sheila spoke of the drawings children make to

illustrate Gospel stories, drawings that are local in every way. "I recall one of Our Lord sitting on the steps of a nipa-thatched home talking to Mary Magdalen, both of them Filipinos. Around their feet played little Filipino chickens and little Filipino pigs."

A Filipino student is bombarded with languages. "At our college a student uses English in the classroom but speaks Visayan at home and between classes. All the while he is studying Spanish and Tagalog, the national language. Taking this in consideration, it is remarkable that they do so well in English. Of course, the inevitable howlers come along when the speech habits of one language carry over into another. But once you get to know that 'p' and 'f' are interchangeable in Visayan you know exactly what a student means when he tells you he will practice 'finance' for Lent."

Sister Mary Sheila felt that the wonderful thing about being a teacher in the Philippines is that one is appealing to people whose response to spiritual ideals is immediate and eager. "They are hungering for something that you have to give them. If you weren't there, many of them would have to do without."

Patrick Cronin has long been aware of this hunger. How to reach people who are no longer apt to sit in a classroom? He returned from the Vatican Council in Rome feeling that a broadcasting station was a partial answer to that question. Such a station could help educate the Filipinos now that nearly every family owns a cheap transistor radio. The programs could reach nearly three million people with a signal covering six provinces. The archbishop saw radio as a more useful medium than newspapers or magazines because many people in Mindanao are illiterate.

Radio could keep people alert to what is happening locally and in the world. Educational and entertainment programs might develop such themes as justice, charity, and the dignity of man. The possibilities for instruction in homemaking, nutrition, and child care were unending.

From his work in the hills, the bishop knew that when poor people get sick they cannot afford a doctor and often consult a local medicine man whose remedies can do more harm than good. He felt sure that several excellent local doctors would volunteer to broadcast simple instructions in the elementary treatment of common ills.

The Columbans built the station with $25,000 of borrowed money. A surplus secondhand army transmitter cost $2,500 and a used tower turned up at a bargain. Fortunately, a Filipino who is a technical genius kept the dilapidated equipment operating when all odds seemed against it. He accomplished this with the great native patience that had helped Colonel Fertig get messages on the air in wartime.

No sooner was station DXDD on the air than programs began to develop out of a felt need. For example, one day a college student said to Sean Coyle, "Father, what's a Beethoven?"

Father Coyle figured there were many more people who did not know what a Beethoven was, and so he said to the station manager, "Why don't we have a program of classical music?"

The manager said, "Why not? You do it. When do you want to start?"

The next Sunday night Father Coyle started presenting everything from Romberg to Rachmaninoff from Grieg to Gershwin. Soon the program was picked up by DYRF, a station run by the Irish Redemptorists in Cebu City.

Again, Father Coyle approached the station manager, "Why don't we have a program presented by students?"

The manager answered, "Great! I can't give you money, but I can give you time on the air and a technician."

When the young priest and his students found that they needed help, the station manager came to the rescue. He arranged for Father James Reuter, S.J., to come for a week during the summer vacation to give a workshop in radio drama production.

"We literally sweated the week out," said Father Coyle. "The airconditioning in the recording studio, where we spent most of our time, was out of order. And believe me, Ozamis can be hot in June. We produced six plays. Father Reuter directed the first and students directed the rest. We were on the way."

The programming developed gradually until now the station is on the air from 5 A.M. until 10 P.M. Much of the news, taken from the Voice of America and the BBC World Report, is translated into native dialects. A great deal of drama is still written and performed by local talent. Many hours are filled with farm news, pop tunes, and roundtable discussions about such things as education, liturgy, and family planning.

Anyone with an emergency call can broadcast it whenever DXDD is on the air. This service got started because there are no telephone or telegraph services extending to the distant *barrios.* One of the most popular programs is on the air from seven to eight each morning, an hour when anyone with a personal message can come into the studio and broadcast it.

Sometimes a student calls a far-off *barrio* with a plea to his family to send money or rice. Or a distraught father from a mountain village begs his runaway daughter to come home. Many times the visitor in the studio is a traveler informing his folks that he will be a day or two late because of a storm at sea.

Shortly before leaving Ozamis, in 1970, Archbishop Cronin turned over to the diocese the radio station which had just been built by the Columbans. The new bishop, Jesus Y. Varela, put the station under the management of a layman who works under direction of a diocesan board.

The hierarchy in the Philippines seems to have made a wise decision when it set a parochial school system as the number one priority. Even though some public school principals allowed brief religious instruction outside of regular class time, the bishops knew that this was not really religious education. So they put their stress on starting schools, and good results followed.

They found that Catholic schools helped the missionary do what he is supposed to do: work himself out of a job. If enough religious vocations come out of the schools, he can turn over the work to the local clergy and move on. This has happened in the islands where there are many vocations even though a drop in vocations prevails in other parts of the world.

The effect of a school on parish life is dramatic. Statistics bear this out. Father Michael Acton's experience in starting a school is worth studying because it is typical of the headaches and the satisfactions that come from the effort:

When the district of Bacold became a municipality, with its own town council, Father Acton was appointed its first resident pastor. He began by extending the cramped one-room *convento,* renovating the small chapel, and organizing a schedule of monthly Masses in chapels throughout the area.

When he realized that his ministry could be more effective if he had a parish school, he began constructing a simple three-room building. By the time the main posts stood tall and straight against the sky, all funds were exhausted. At this critical moment help came from the bishop, the Columban superior, and friends at home. The roof went on and the walls went up, but furnishing would have to come little by little.

Father Acton grew thin and sunburnt, working all day with the carpenters and tossing beneath a mosquito net at night worrying about the next step. He knew that a nearby school had asked the Department of Education not to grant him a permit to begin classes. Even though the town mayor and the local parliamentary deputy asked for the permit the department was reluctant. In Father Acton's case the department finally granted a permit after receiving a petition from hundreds of parents.

When the new school opened its doors that June to the first and second year students, the missionary was confronted with new problems. He found himself with 174 students instead of the maximum of 120 he had expected. So before the door was open he needed more classrooms and more equipment.

Suddenly his church was also too small. He said, "My Sunday Mass attendance tripled as soon as I started the school." That was the day the young priest knew that the bishops had shown wisdom in their priorities.

19 ✣ Nutribuns and Bananas

When a young priest comes into the *convento* looking paper-thin after a stay in the hills, the archbishop asks, "Are you getting enough to eat?" He is aware that food is not always plentiful in Mindanao.

One day Sister Esperanza arrived at the *convento* saying that she had pigs to deliver to three eagerly waiting tenant farmers but lacked transportation. The archbishop saw this as food that needed to be delivered right away to where it could do the most good, so he offered the little Filipina sister the use of his car knowing full well that pigs as passengers don't improve the resale value.

Sister Esperanza went lurching down the road in the episcopal automobile, but alas, upon arrival at the *barrio* one pig was missing. It had jumped to freedom. The nun walked back over the three miles sounding pig calls all the way and telling her troubles to all she met. She didn't find the pig that day but her efforts were rewarded three days later when the prodigal was given to its new owner.

Nothing pleases the archbishop more than hearing Columbans solving a food problem in an imaginative way. For example, when Father Marcus Keyes was stationed in Iligan he started a program to fight malnutrition, as did Father Joseph Shiels in Lopez Jaena.

Father Keyes improved the health of his parish with nutribuns. Each of the small loaves, a little larger than a hamburger bun, contains all nutrients found in a glass of milk and tastes good, too.

Up until 1973 the children in Iligan went hungry. It was then that Father Keyes, visiting one of the world's worst slums, the Tondo in Manila, saw the wonders nutribuns were working for 100,000 children there.

Upon returning to Iligan he was more haunted than ever by the sight of a hungry child because now he knew how to solve the problem but couldn't afford to. He made a plea to readers of the Columban magazine, *Columban Mission,* and the result was immediate and amazing.

With money coming from generous readers, Father Keyes installed modern baking equipment at the Catholic Social Service Center and gathered a dedicated staff under the direction of Sister Rosario, a Mercy sister. The United States Catholic Relief services agreed to provide the flour free. The penny the school children pay helps cover some of the cost of powdered milk and other ingredients, the upkeep of the trucks, and the salaries of the bakers.

The program was hardly begun when 30,000 nutribuns were being baked daily for 63 schools. Suddenly the number was cut back to 27,000 when United States AID's surplus grain allotment dropped, making less flour available to Catholic Relief Services.

In many villages the most exciting event of the day is the arrival of the nutribun truck. The children watch for it with eagerness because for many the buns are the best meal of the day, and for some the only meal. If there is a breakdown and delivery is delayed, it is a minor crisis at the school. Drivers of the three ancient, battered trucks are greeted on their rounds with the cry of "Nutribun! Nutribun! Nutribun!"

In the fight against malnutrition, Father Joseph Shiels used a different method. His 17,000 parishioners at Lopez Jaena are mostly sharecropping coconut farmers earning less than a dollar a day.

How to take care of their malnourished children was a question that caused the young Columban many a sleepless night. The answer came to him the day a friend made him a gift of a bunch of Lakatan bananas. As Father Shiels watched the school children eat the bananas with delight he decided to get the farmers to grow Lakatans.

In studying the banana-growing, Father Shiels discovered that the Lakatan root can be separated into sets, much like onion or garlic sets. Each of the seven or eight sets per root can be replanted and in turn reproduce seven or eight more. So a nursery can develop easily.

Father Shiels invested ten dollars in a hundred plants to start a pilot nursery. He sent two young men to the Del Monte Experimental School to learn about banana-growing. They returned to report that bananas require careful cultivation and that a *carabao*-drawn plow can't do the job properly. So the missionary turned to his friends for a hand-guided motor tiller, which plows more in one day than a *carabao* can in six, and for a power pump to water and spray plants.

Before long, 100,000 banana trees were growing in the parish. The farmers of Lopez-Jaena soon doubled their incomes, and malnutrition was on the wane.

Out of this great concern for better nutrition has come Nati. Her story is worth telling as an example of how things get done under austere conditions. Instead of a complex bureaucracy planning a funded program, a few dedicated individuals such as Nati take up the burden and work wonders.

In telling of her achievements, Father William Hannafin, the pastor of San Roque, in Iligan City, said, *"Asa man si Nati?* Where is Nati? That's all I hear no matter where I travel in my vast 'city' parish which is mostly country."

Unless the young priest happens to be in the same *barrio* with her he doesn't know where the lithe, intense Nati is. She travels so fast and furiously that her pastor cannot keep track of her, much less keep up with her.

Nati, baptized Natividad Casillano, is in charge of the nutrition program in San Roque's parish. The 700 malnourished children in her care are scattered in little *barrios* back in the mountains where there is not even a jeep trail, so Nati often travels by foot carrying her burden of supplies.

A mountain woman walked from one of the distant hills to Iligan City to demand of Father Hannafin, "Where is Nati?" Before he could answer she poured out her well-prepared plea, telling about all the children who are sick, and the mothers who need advice, and the old people who need care. She had not met Nati but the mountain grapevine carried the news of the wonders she works. The hill woman ended her outburst by demanding once again, "Where is Nati?"

Fortunately for the young priest, the popular Natividad Casillano was at home base that morning weighing the children of the neighborhood and instructing their parents.

Before starting to work for San Roque's parish, Nati had served for a time as a social worker. In college she majored in home economics and had begun work toward an M.A. in nutrition when her money ran out. She hopes some day to return to college for her degree.

Nati's whirlwind day begins at 7:30 A.M. in her small office in the *convento*. After some book work she sees callers for an hour and then sets off to one of the *barrios*. There a group of helpers gather parents together for a lecture. This might be on nutrition, baby care, or advice to pregnant mothers. Sometimes Nati gives a cooking demonstration showing how local foods and AID foods can be used together.

About noon she returns to the office, has a hurried lunch, and catches up on some paper work. By two o'clock she is off again to another *barrio* for a repeat performance. Sometimes the afternoon is devoted to house-to-house visits, the most important part of the program, she says, because it involves the personal touch and all kinds of problems can be discussed.

Then there are the children—700 of them from six months to five years old who must be checked and weighed and charted each month. Volunteers are a great help in this, but Nati personally cares for the children who are severly malnourished.

Father Hannafin said, "Sometimes I go along and it is amazing to see the interest she has aroused and how anxious people are to help. She never lacks for willing volunteers. Nati has learned a lot from experience. She keeps lectures short and simple and uses many charts, pictures, color slides, and posters. In the cooking demonstration, I notice she is turning more and more to local foods making the AID foods supplementary, since that supply will be phased out. Nati has started printing simple recipes so that parents will cook foods in a way that retains nutrition."

Father Hannafin believes that the secret of Nati's success is that she is so dedicated, so enthusiastic. She has learned to identify with the people she serves. When she shows women how to prepare meals they go home and try it just because Nati said they should. The poor accept food from her without feeling it is a handout. They see her as one of them, sharing with them. She doesn't make them feel poor.

The Columbans never become accustomed to the sight of undernourished children even though large numbers of them lack a proper diet. The experience is especially traumatic when missionaries come upon hunger that verges on starvation. Father Michael Cullen will never forget his first experience with prolonged hunger.

"It couldn't have happened at a worse time. The jeep disintegrated just as the rice shortage hit our island. The rice shortage was causing suffering because the substitute crop, corn, was still two months from harvest.

"The jeep's demise left me afoot with many a mile of plain and mountain to cover. Worse, still, I couldn't haul the meager supplies to those who needed them most. But I could go myself."

Father Cullen and Julio, the parish clerk, set off at four o'clock one morning for a village in the remote and lonely mountains of the hinterland. They took a bus down the coast road to the next town and then waited for a motorcycle with a sidecar to take them five miles to the river. While waiting in front of a grocery, the lady who owned the place asked where they were going. When she heard the name of the village she muttered what seemed a prayer and said, "It will kill you, Father. There isn't even rice here in town—there's nothing up there."

When she realized that the two were determined to go she rushed off and grabbed the first food she could lay hands on—five eggs and a small packet of biscuits. She insisted the men take them as *balon,* food for the road.

After many breakdowns the motorcycle finally carried the priest and his clerk to the river. The two of them forded the swollen stream and began the three-hour trek to the village. Monsoon rains had made the trails almost impassable with mud and water. The men crossed three other rivers swollen by the rains.

When Father Cullen and Julio arrived at the village chapel, the parishioners came pouring in from all over the hill country. A short refresher course in the basic teachings of Christianity was followed by confessions, Mass, more instruction, and baptisms.

"Then we sat around and discussed current events, especially the rice shortage. When conversation seemed exhausted one man did what all Filipinos dread; he said, 'Sorry Father, there isn't a bite in the village, not even a little corn.' I said it didn't matter;

we weren't really hungry. Nothing can minimize the loss of face a Filipino suffers when he cannot entertain a visitor with food.

"Then I remembered the *balon,* and suggested we eat it now. This gave relief all around. Soon the five eggs were hard-boiled and offered to us. We had to take one apiece. It would be unforgivable to refuse. Then we divided the biscuits and the other three eggs among the children."

As they sat there on the ground taking small bites and chewing thoroughly, trying to make the food last, an old woman said, "Father, we old ones can resist the hunger. Our problem is the children. They cry all night with hunger. They can't understand why there is no food."

The two visitors tightened their belts and set off on another, long and hungry journey. Down to the river they went and in no time were lost from view among the tall cogan grass. Soon Father Cullen felt faint and sat down.

"In such circumstances one must think," he says. "Plan. Do something. But what? I had seen plenty of malnutrition, but never before had I seen hunger that I could do nothing about. I looked toward the faraway mountain range. Our eventual goal was a village seven hours away. We would stop at a nearer one for the night."

The two men tightened their belts another notch and hiked on. After crossing several mountain ranges and rivers they reached a village at dusk. There was food, but not much.

"I'll never forget the delicious meal of *camoti* cooked with salt and water," Father Cullen recalled. "It's of the potato family. The villagers were profuse in their apologies for not having rice. I think they didn't believe me when I explained that in my country the potato is a staple food.

"They gathered in the hundreds for the Mass and sacraments. It had been many years since a priest had reached them. Not since the time of Father John Doohan. His name, ten years later, is still a household word there."

Next morning Father Cullen and Julio left the village to cross more mountains, more rivers. On the way to the village of their destination they came upon a small chapel in which had been placed a statue of Santo Nino. Father Cullen wanted to push on to make the village before dark, knowing that the last cliff rising from the river is very steep, almost a thousand feet.

The people pleaded with the priest to rest an hour or two. He sat on a log, so very tired, and within fifteen minutes a large crowd had gathered from houses not visible because they were tucked in the crevices of the cliffs or hidden deep in uncleared forests.

"I asked them if they would like Mass. They were delighted. The children had never seen a priest nor attended a Mass. Julio explained it to them while I heard confessions. When Mass was over they insisted I have refreshment. *Camoti* again, and again it tasted delicious."

As Father Cullen moved among the crowd he overheard an old man say: *"Salamat as Dios, Naga ohao kami para sa Santos nga Misa!"* (Thanks be to God, we were thirsty for the Holy Mass!) That one sentence brought him a poignant realization: a missionary has two hungers demanding his attention—when he thinks only of one or the other he is not in touch with reality.

20 ✢ Medics on the Move

A rchbishop Cronin is pleased that the Knights of Columbus have established clinics in his cathedral parish and in San Antonio parish. He is proud of Maria Reyna hospital, conducted by the Sisters of St. Paul de Chartres in his cathedral city of Cagayan de Oro. Yet he realizes that fifty beds and a staff of twelve sisters are inadequate for an archdiocese that numbers nearly 700,000 people.

Often on his trips to the *barrios* the archbishop sees enough illness to make him sick at heart. Too often he hears stories such as the one about Juanita told by Sister Rosemary, of the Sisters of Mercy of Lanao, a foundation of the Mercy Sisters of Buffalo, N.Y.

When the sister asked Juanita how long she had been coughing blood, the frail fifteen-year-old dropped her head in shame and said, "For more than a year." When asked if she felt any pain she pointed to her chest. Has she told her mother? She said she lives with an aunt because both parents are dead.

Sister Rosemary wanted Juanita to have a chest examination but there were no facilities for diagnosis in Kolambugan. So she took the girl across the bay to Ozamis City where a fluoroscopy was followed by a doctor's examination. Ninety-five percent of Juanita's left lung was tubercular.

When the aunt heard about this she put the sick girl out of the house saying she might infect the other children. This is one of the reasons Filipinos are reluctant to come for an examination; they try to avoid having the bad news become official, for once it does they are apt to be shunned by relatives and friends. Fortunately, Juanita was able to persuade another aunt in Ozamis City to take pity on her.

Sister Rosemary told the girl that even though she enjoyed being busy she would have to stop all strenuous activity for the time being. The nursing sisters find it difficult to make patients realize the importance of rest, and Juanita was more difficult to convince than most. Inactivity hurt her more than the daily injection of streptomycin. The sisters also gave her a supply of isoniazid medicine and instructed her in good nutritional and good health habits. In time Juanita gained weight and her beautiful complexion returned.

Thousands of such cases are found in the Philippines where tuberculosis is the number one killer. The two factors that contribute most to this are poor nutrition and unsanitary conditions.

Much of the fight against disease in Mindanao must be carried on by individuals, such as Sister Rosemary, or by small volunteer teams similar to those in Oroquieta and Gingoog. The Oroquieta group, formed by the Knights of Columbus, meets at noon each Sunday at the *convento*. There is much hustle and bustle as medicines and personnel are checked for a visit to a *barrio*.

Five doctors, a dozen nurses and several volunteer helpers stack into jeeps and trucks boxes of medicine, sacks of cornmeal, a public address system, and a record player.

The village may be three miles away, or it may be fifteen. In benign weather the team will have an easy trip, but when rain falls the roads are so bad that everybody has to get out and push.

Upon arrival at the *barrio* the team shatters the quiet of the afternoon by sending across the public address system the beat of Ricky Nelson or The Beatles, music not meant to entertain but to announce that the clinic is ready for business. People begin to gather at one of the bigger *barrio* houses where the doctors examine patients.

The most common ailments are worms, beriberi, sores of various sorts, and obo, a cough which is generally a symptom of tuberculosis. Most of the diseases stem from malnutrition. Babies and very young children are the usual victims. Some babies are so deformed from undernourishment that they look less than human.

As the work goes on, a nurse hands out vitamin pills, and another wishes she had more drugs for the tubercular. A doctor examines a child who will not cooperate; another listens to an old lady protesting that she has been given only tablets instead of the more highly esteemed injections.

While observing this commotion, Father Patrick Fahey said,

"Surely nowhere this side of heaven will you find patience to equal that of the Philippine medical profession!"

By evening from fifty to a hundred people have been treated. One member of the team gives a short talk on hygiene. As a parting gift every patient receives a bag of cornmeal. To the strains of "Lover's Guitar" the villagers make their way homeward through the coconut groves, and the medical team relaxes over a cup of coffee before starting the return journey.

In Gingoog town the Columbans organized fourteen volunteers into a team which included doctors, nurses, midwives, and students who help with the paper work. The team visits 47 villages in a parish of 37,000 people.

During the visits doctors perform minor surgery but mainly they distribute medicine. They give special attention to children under twelve, the group that accounts for seventy percent of the deaths, caused largely by respiratory and gastrointestinal diseases. A simple ailment such as the common cold is often fatal because of a lack of resistance and a lack of the most elementary medicine.

Thanks to Sister Frances Daly, a Columban who directed the clinic in Ozamis, the medicines distributed are free ever since she asked for samples from pharmaceutical firms in the Philippines, United States, Ireland, and Australia. Since patients have an average income of not much more than a dollar a day, they would not be able to afford to pay for medication. An ancient Filipino asked a Columban priest about the costs of medicine in America, and when told, said, "It's cheaper to have a funeral than to get sick!"

Archbishop Cronin's old parish in remote Molave once had twenty doctors visit it from Manila. All at once! Dr. Barnes, the head of Far Eastern University's medical mission institute, accepted an invitation from Father Eamon Fleming to visit his parishioners in the mountains of Mindanao.

The Philipines Air Force flew the twenty doctors free of charge the 500 miles from Manila to Ozamis City. There Father Robert Stack took care of their transport by jeep the remaining fifty miles. In Molave, Fathers Fleming and William Smith housed eight at the *convento* and the rest with neighbors in the town.

"We had, of course, given notice to the parishioners of their coming," said Father Fleming. "Minor operations were performed daily at the presbytery. From Thursday through Saturday groups of doctors traveled around the villages giving free drugs, treatment, and advice. On Sunday the whole team worked at the presbytery, converted into a field hospital with four clinics and one operating theatre."

Dr. Barnes, the leader of the mission, was kicked in the ankle by his horse on his first outing to a village, and thereafter he was confined to headquarters, where he continued to supervise. Dr. Villafria, the surgeon, had a busy time excising cysts and tumors, performing minor eye operations, and drawing fluid from patients suffering from schistosomiasis, a disease peculiar to the East and common in the Philippines. It is caused by a snail which enters the body through the feet and works its way into the stomach. It is generally fatal.

By the time the doctors departed on Monday they had treated 2,500 patients.

"Perhaps the most important thing," said Father Fleming, "is what they did for the spirit. They impressed the whole parish with their spirit at work, their cheerfulness, and their good nature."

Although Mindanao is a tropical island it already knows the ills of industrialism. For example, industry has brought its social problems to Iligan, a city of 100,000 with no unemployment compensation, no care for the disabled, no public housing. In every city in the Philippines, there are problems caused by an inadequate water supply, lack of disposal, congested living, and racketeering landlords.

While describing how people live below human standards in Iligan City, Father John Chute said: "One day on my visitation I met Catalino Mattalaba, a leper who lived in a broken down shack with his wife and nine children. It was pathetic to see them in indescribable filth and want. He couldn't work because he had no fingers or toes, and his wife worked at the market as a fish-seller's helper for fifty cents a day. We collected a few wooden boxes from some Chinese businessmen and brought some nipa for the roof. Jose, a carpenter, volunteered his services, and at a minimal cost we fixed up a small, wooden one-room house for Catalino."

After this many people began to haunt Father Chute for help.

Felipe, a mental defective, lived in a pigpen down by the water-front. With some scraps of timber that were lying around the rectory, Jose and a helper built him a clean wooden shack.

The mayor of Mahayahay donated a building lot and Father Chute and Jose built a house on it for an abandoned wife with four children. Next they completed a house for a tubercular and his family. After building one for a deaf and dumb man, they constructed in rapid succession a house for a widow with two children, one for a vendor and his family, and one for a family whose children were contaminated with all sorts of sores. Nine houses were built at a cost of approximately fifty dollars each.

In the middle of all of this congestion, the Franciscan Missionaries of Mary opened a dispensary in Saray, a slum, and the Catholic Women's League opened another at the back of the church.

Along with the new health problems brought about by industry, many of the indigenous ones still remain. For example, a *manangiti,* a coconut tree climber, usually dies young. If he avoids a fall and consequent death or disablement, or resists being snared into alcoholism from *tuba* drinking, he invariably ends up with a damaged heart from the strain of climbing a half mile straight up every day.

A Columban tells of one of his parishioners who twice a day climbs thirty-four trees, averaging from forty to forty-five feet in height, to collect two gallons of *tuba* that sells for about twenty-five cents a gallon. *Tuba,* which the *manangiti* taps from the stem of the palm frond at the top, is a sweet and potent drink in its raw state, and becomes palm wine when fermented.

The missionary said, "With respect and fascination I watched Ricardo work. The curved knife which he carried at his hip in a carved, wooden holster was locally forged and honed to a razor edge. A bamboo container slung over his shoulder has two simple attachments. One was an ingenious homemade bamboo brush for cleaning residue in the smaller containers attached to the tree into which the *tuba* drips overnight. The other was a small coconut shell, shiny with age and use, in which he carried the red powdered bark of the *burok* tree, an additive mixed with the *tuba* to give it a beerlike tang.

"Climbing can be an arduous and ungainly process, but Ricardo, effortlessly swaying himself upward, zigzagging from one notched foothold to another, made it look like waltzing. Afterward, when there was no one watching, I tried it and became glued to the trunk with fright at the fourth notch. Unable to go up or down, I had to hang on until Ricardo came along to rescue me."

Although missionaries see to it that medical care reaches hundreds of *barrios,* there are thousands in which no medical doctor has ever set foot. When people in those remote areas become sick they seek relief from the *herbolario* found in every village. The *herbolario,* either man or woman, mixes roots, herbs, and plants for healing. Some for external use, some for internal. Millions of people are born and die without ever having anyone other than the herb doctor to turn to in time of sickness. In such villages there are many deaths during the first three years of life.

21 ✦ Body and Soul

Social services have increased in Mindanao since Patrick Cronin arrived forty years ago. They are social services with a difference. As the archbishop explains, a missionary needs to care about the hunger of spiritual poverty as well as the hunger of material poverty—body and soul. This is in line with the teaching of Saint Thomas Aquinas that a sufficiency of the goods of the world is needed for the practice of virtue.

Describing these programs is difficult because there are so many and they are usually small and fashioned to fit the special need of a specific parish. Maybe this is best made clear, and the variety of the work suggested, by letting three Columbans—Fathers John Chute, Hugh O'Halpin, and Donald Kill—speak of their experience in developing programs.

Father Chute took a special interest in the people of the *baybay* (shoreline). These fishermen, tough, hardy, cheerful, are usually very poor. In a struggle for existence they farm the sea in their frail *bancas.*

"Walk along any *baybay* in the Philippines," said Father Chute "and you'll see nipa shacks built on stilts, fishermen mending their nets, women washing clothes by the side of a well, and swarms of children barefoot and ragged. The fishermen go out every night and return at sunrise. Fishing is a form of sharecropping here; the owner of the boat, usually a business man downtown, gets one third, and the fishermen get the rest."

When the husband goes to sleep, his wife goes off to market to sell the fish. The fisherman's share on a good night could be two dollars; on a bad night, forty cents; and during bad weather, zero. With this he supports his wife and as many as ten children.

"Everything about their lives is minimal," said Father Chute. "A few mats on which the family sleeps together, a cooking pot, a box for clothes, a few aluminum plates, and a jar for water— that's all. At dinner they squat on the floor eating boiled rice and dried fish with their bare hands. Most can't spare money for shoes. They wear sandals and their clothes are patched and repatched. The children are born without an attending doctor or midwife. When sick there is no money for medicine. Few children finish grade school. They start young helping their fathers at sea."

What is the Church in Lanao province doing for the people of the *baybay?* Many priests help individual fishermen's families in time of sickness by supplying medicine. The Franciscan Missionaries of Mary have a clinic in Saray Baybay and the Mercy Sisters have a mobile clinic. Many of the fishermen belong to parish credit unions in the various coastal towns. Since the population explosion is really felt on the *baybay,* there are three natural family-planning clinics now being operated by the Church in Lanao.

"All of this is only a beginning," said Father Chute. "Much more needs to be done in evangelization and development. Now is the time for the Church to do what Christ did—serve the poorest of the poor."

Father O'Halpin's concern has been with the farmers. For years he tried unsuccessfully to get the tenants near Ozamis to plant second crops under the coconut trees. Finally he asked the Peace Corps to send someone with training in agriculture, hoping that an expert might succeed where he had failed.

"They sent Jim Kern," said Father O'Halpin. "He moved in quietly with no fuss, no 'let's get the ball rolling,' nearly three years ago. He said he'd need some land to plant seedlings. The only land we had was a new cemetery, so he planted in the unused parts. He asked if he could borrow the jeep to go up in the mountain, he needed some samples of earth to send to Manila for analysis."

That was the beginning—slow, careful, asking about the land, having it tested, consulting experts, checking the markets. Jim decided on coffee plants for the unused land under the coconut trees. Coffee, he felt, had the best prospects for growth, income, and market.

The seeds were planted in plastic bags filled with earth in a nursery. In the first six months 40,000 coffee plants were sent to the *barrios* for distribution. Soon 100,000 plants a month were sent out. Beforehand, some of Jim's coworkers had gone to those *barrios* to give seminars on coffee culture. They continue sending instructions to the farmers over the radio station built by the Columbans with donations from friends in the United States.

"Meanwhile back at the cemetery," said Father O'Halpin. "This unobtrusive man has quietly taken over most of it. Where to bury the dead is beginning to be our problem. He has planted the best kind of every vegetable growable and established an extensive seed bank. These seeds are in continual demand by the farmers. They see it as better food for the children and a way of increasing a meager income.

"Jim Kearn uses his Peace Corps salary to pay his four or five workers. He even gave up smoking to save a little money. Most of the expenses on this project are paid by Jim and his parents in Pennsylvania. To the Peace Corps we say, 'Thank you,' and to Jim Kern we say, 'Can't you stay a little longer among us?' "

Father Kill told of how one beautiful gesture of his parishioners in Aurora was like a pebble dropped in water, setting up a rippling effect that has touched more people than anyone could have foreseen, and it continues on and on. The beautiful gesture was the welcoming and feeding of refugees. From this act grew the Social Action Committee whose work continues even though the crisis is past.

The refugees were from burned-out towns destroyed by insurgent guerrilla activity and Christian-Muslim fighting. When they arrived the people of Aurora, desperately poor themselves, gave all they had. To complicate matters their only cash crop, coconuts, failed.

"If we wanted to survive we had to organize," said Father Kill. "We saw how our Diocese of Pagadian cared for refugees through its Social Action Committee directed by Father Warren Ford. Our first need was for food, that was evident, so we started a social action team of our own and our first program was called 'Food for Work'. It's based on the belief that no matter how poor a man is, he more easily maintains his dignity if he is able to work for whatever he is given."

To start with, the parishioners and the refugees began cultivating the land around the church in Aurora. They worked so hard that the city council was sufficiently impressed to offer them the land around the municipal buildings. The result was a three-acre town garden.

"The people worked as long and as hard as they could, and in return received an allowance of rice and corn, with a little money to buy other necessities," said Father Kill. "But there were still more problems in Aurora. A lack of enough good food was beginning to show on the children. We took 500 of them to the provincial hospital for examination and found that 185 suffered from malnutrition."

Father Kill and his committee realized it is more humane and less expensive to give away nutritional food than to buy expensive medicines for sickly children, so they adopted a plan already in use in Mindanao. They built a single oven in the parish hall to bake nutribuns, the meal-in-a-bun described earlier.

Food continued to be a concern even after the refugees had gone. The failure of the coconut crop meant the farmers had to depend for food and cash on their only other crop—corn. The corn crop of Aurora isn't of high quality; in fact, the poor soil and hilly land would cause an American farmer to throw up his hands in despair.

Since corn is a seasonal crop, the farmer is at the mercy of corn buyers who buy the harvest at about five cents for 2.2 pounds and hold it until the price triples. Then they sell it back to the farmer at a time when he must either buy or starve.

"Without cash from their coconuts the farmers can't buy food when the corn supply gives out. They can't buy fertilizer, either. And they have to pay an outrageous 125 percent on money they borrow."

To rescue farmers from corn buyers and usurers, the Aurora Social Action Committee started a corn bank. This cooperative buys corn, stores it, and sells it back at a just price when farmers need it most. Whatever is left is sold outside the community. All money is plowed back into the community in the form of low interest loans for seed and fertilizer.

Father Kill has contacted farmers in his native Ohio to learn better tilling and growing techniques. He is also trying to grow another crop of something during the year to get more use out of the land. In the midst of such activity he has started a school that teaches handicrafts and sewing so that his parishioners might supplement a meager income. All of this sprung from a Social Action Committee that was started as part of a beautiful gesture at the time the refugees arrived.

Patrick Cronin, when still a young missionary, realized that "man does not live by bread alone" is more than a quotable quote with a nice ring to it. He realized that to offer bread and not be resented he must never forget the deeper hunger. Material help and spiritual concern have to go hand-in-hand. In this double concern, the work of missionaries differs from that of state social services.

22 ✢ Head of the Wise Crows

When dedicating the St. Joseph's Family Center at Ozamis, in June of 1967, Bishop Cronin felt the importance of the new organization and said so. He used the occasion to express his gratitude for the wonderful things the sisters had done in Mindanao, acknowledging that the work of the Columban priests and certainly his own, would have been impoverished without them.

The remarkable achievement of the sisters deserves a book of its own; here we can only hint at it. In confining their story to a few pages, it may be best told through the work of one of them, Sister Breda Noonan.

Typical of Sister Breda's experiences is one that happened at dusk as she and Sister Mary Rosalie were on their way home. They were hurrying because night comes down suddenly in the tropics and they were still in the slums of Ozamis.

A little girl came running to them begging, "Please come to my house!"

The nuns hesitated until they learned that the girl was the eldest daughter of Juan, a patient at the clinic who was suffering from advanced tuberculosis. They felt uneasy crossing a long, sagging plank that barely kept their feet clear of the slime and stagnant water covering the pathway. Upon reaching the girl's 'home' the sisters found a one-room shack, six by ten feet, where Juan lived with his wife, Leonila, and seven children.

The four smallest children were lying sick on the bare floor. Juan, too ill and too weak to work, had gone to the neighbors to ask for food; sometimes Leonila could not earn enough for one meal a day. The rent had not been paid for months and now the family was about to be evicted. The heaviness of despondency filled the fetid air inside the crowded room.

The nuns left a few pesos for food. On their way back to St. Joseph's Family Center they resolved that somehow, someday, Juan's family would have a real home.

Soon things began to happen. First of all, new parish equipment arrived packed in twenty-three crates. Wooden crates would make good walls for a house! With funds donated by friends at home, the nuns were able to buy wood for the framework and nipa for the roof. Local families gave bamboo. Juan gathered together his friends and in a surprisingly short time they had built a new home.

"When I went to visit them," said Sister Breda, "it was unbelievable what a difference it made. Juan and Leonila were transformed people. I noticed that the packing crates had been stenciled, 'Society of St. Columban.' There was no money for such a luxury as paint and so the house bears these words like a banner."

Now they had a decent home, but how could they support themselves? In Ozamis work is not easy to find even for able-bodied men, and for one weakened from the effects of TB it is practically impossible.

Through the credit union at St. Joseph's Center, Juan obtained a loan to finance a home garden. Hard work, which involved even the smallest children, made the project productive. Slowly the family found its way to the self-respect that comes through living with dignity.

In the sisters' clinic it is not only the sick who are sitting in the waiting room of the clinic when the nuns arrive in the morning. As one nun said, "Everyone is here to share something—their sorrows or their joys. Mrs. Sumalinog is here again this morning. A few months ago she was sharing her sorrows when suddenly widowed and left alone to care for five small children, with a new baby on the way, and no home, and no income. With a loan from the Family Center's credit union she gradually developed a small store, selling only bananas at first, but now she offers a variety of foods. Another loan helped her build a room behind the store."

When her baby was born, she was completely supported by the Family Center and supplied with food. Now she is independent and proud of it. Today she is here to share her joy. Last week she even offered shelter to a woman who was also suddenly widowed and left without a home or support.

The work of the sisters has a recurring theme: find people who are down, help them lurch up onto the road, and point them in the direction of hope and dignity. If the nuns can't find jobs for these people, they make them. One way they do this is by starting cottage industries.

Raising turkeys is one such. Since turkeys are still strangers in Ozamis, and in all of the Philippines, they have attracted comment and attention. The Soft Toy Project is another cottage industry. Women are working full time at the Family Center making teddy bears, blue wooly dogs, and rabbits with button eyes. And Sister Breda added, "Don't forget the traditional mickey mouses. Or should I say mickey mice?"

A nursery school has been modeled after Project Headstart in the United States. "It's one more weapon against crippling poverty and sickness. Our preschoolers are a delightful addition to the 'family' at the Center. A visit to their classroom is a sure cure for Monday morning blues."

Archbishop Cronin is pleased that the sisters are giving more and more attention to youth these days. He and the nuns are aware that forty-seven percent of the population in the Philippines are fifteen years old or younger. He points out that, while the figure of forty-seven percent is cold and lifeless, the reality on which it is based is anything but cold and lifeless.

To describe the reality, Sister Breda told of the evening the sisters were showing a film in a poor neighborhood. "We decided to show it outside so that a greater number could attend. This forty-seven percent came alive dramatically! We had to stop the projector because of the teeming, pressing, reckless, youthful audience. We just couldn't cope.

"Perhaps that's the best way to sum up our feelings at the moment—we cannot cope. Young, uneducated, poverty-stricken children press us from all sides. We know that the hope of tomorrow lies in them, but their energy and potential go untapped. It's all idly or viciously wasted."

Sister Breda is always specific. She has faced up to enough problems in her time to realize that life is not lived as glittering generalities but as one specific instance after another. And so, when she speaks of her concern for the future of the young, she speaks of some specific young people—Roberto, Luz, and Bernardo.

Roberto lives in a slum, the third of twelve children—eighteen if you include stepbrothers and stepsisters. His father is not often at home because he is constantly looking for work as a log cutter. His eldest sister is married and shares the home along with her husband and six-month-old baby. The home, built through the help of the Columban sisters, consists of one room and a tiny kitchen—rather difficult to find lying-down space at night, but they all seem to manage.

Roberto is thirteen and should be in grade four but, because of continual absences from school, he still struggles with grade two. It is not that he lacks intelligence. He is exceptionally bright as evidenced by his skill at gambling. But his mother has no time or energy to see that he attends school, and the school authorities won't say anything because they have too many problems with those who do attend.

Roberto shines shoes to make a few centavos for the cinema or for gambling. He doesn't think too much about what life may have to offer him. Just enough for today is his policy.

Bernardo is a little older. His mother died leaving his father and seven children to care for themselves. The father suffers from TB. Luz, who is a little younger than Bernardo, is really twelve but she looks eight. She tries to manage the house. Cooking is no problem because there is usually only rice, if that.

"I first came to know Luz," said Sister Breda, "when she stood shyly at the door of the Center one morning. She asked if there was any food available. They hadn't eaten for more than a day. I went to see their 'home' and found it to be a single room, about six-feet square, of rather shaky sticks. I decided not to venture inside despite their invitation. The sticks looked ready to collapse at the slightest provocation. We gave them some help and they moved into a better shack near us."

Bernardo has only finished grade one and has no preparation at all for making a living. Ozamis offers limited openings for skilled workers and less for unskilled. Unemployment and under-employment is a way of life for many able-bodied men. Younger members of the working force suffer most.

Bernardo now has taken to pumping a pedicab—a taxi that operates like a bicycle—a killing job. Sometimes he makes enough money that his family can eat rice at least once that day.

"What will happen to the Robertos and the Bernardos?" asks Sister Breda. "They press on us from every side. We say we can't cope, but with no skills and no hope, how can *they* cope?"

"Roberto and Bernardo are not yet part of any delinquent gangs. Sooner or later their energies must spill over. With no constructive outlets they will be attracted to destructive outlets. The thrill, the excitment, the companionship—all a part of gang life—are appealing to a boy whose home is only a shack and whose work has no meaning.

"In their neighborhood, stabbings and street fights are common enough. A few nights in jail is often the teen-ager's first contact with seasoned criminals. Soon he is back behind bars for a longer time."

The thought of young men in jail haunted Sister Breda a long time. She didn't do anything about it until two young men came to her office in St. Joseph's Family Center saying they wanted to spend their summer vacation working among the deprived of Ozamis. Both young men, Bart Toledo and Librado Baluarte, were studying for the priesthood.

"This was my chance." she says. Now we could reach out to those desperate young people in jail. I eagerly accepted the offer of these two volunteers."

Bart and Librado found seventeen boys behind bars between the ages of twelve and sixteen. They were pale, hungry, and desperate; most were serving sentences for some sort of theft. The volunteer workers did not confine their attention to the boys but reached out to the family, if there was a family left to be found.

Sister Breda recalls that the youngest boy in the group was Jose de la Cruz, a twelve-year-old in for stealing. The previous week his nine-year-old brother had spent the night in jail for the same thing.

"Their father walks the streets selling sweepstakes tickets and has been in jail himself. The mother, occupied with trying to find ways and means to live, is rarely at home. The children have little except what the neighbors give them.

"Jose is small and malnourished. What will he do when he is

set free? He has learned more tricks while in jail and will probably do the next 'job' better."

The nun recalls that some of the other boys were themselves supporting brothers and sisters. One of them supported a grand-mother—his sole relative.

Bart Toledo said, "The first week in the jail was frustrating. We found the young boys mixed in with the older and more hardened criminals. Since we could only stand the heat and atmosphere inside the cells for about two hours at a time, we felt that our work would be ineffective.

"The warden was cooperative. So was the mayor. Soon we were allowed to take the boys out of jail a few hours each day. We took them to St. Joseph's Center. No guards accompanied us. The boys had little inclination to run away—they had nothing better to run to! Through Sister Breda's influence we got the minors put into separate quarters in the jail."

The delinquents, the two volunteers, and Sister Breda found the first few days at St. Joseph's Center an uneasy experience. The air was taut with tension. And then quite suddenly the apprehension disappeared as the daily program of study, work, and sports was accepted, almost with enthusiasm. The study periods included reading and writing and discussions in which the boys spoke of their families and their own hopes for the future. Leaders in the community came to speak; among them was Father Patrick Crow-ley, the parish priest. Sister Breda was realistic enough to sense that "The most important time of the day was snack time—jail food being what it is."

By the end of the summer the delinquents had so improved that all who came in contact with them noticed it. And the center was much improved too, because the boys had cleaned, painted, and made repairs.

"Healing always involves time," said Sister Breda. "Ten weeks with these boys is only a drop in the ocean. Those weeks did bring home to me the need for a permanent rehabilitation center for boys in trouble."

While developing programs for young people the priests and sisters decided to have a premarriage course for couples whose weddings were in sight. This began in 1967 when a group of married people, a priest, and a nun met regularly to discuss how to help improve family life. In the group were representatives of several professions—nursing, medical, social work, and religious.

In recalling these discussions Sister Breda said, "We often heard the same question, 'Why didn't we hear this five, ten, twenty years ago? *Before* we were married!' These lay people decided to plan a course for young couples about to be married. They realized the need much better than any of us priests or nuns."

While consulting with Bishop Cronin the group decided that the course should be conducted the first three Sunday mornings of the month. The lay members of the board stressed that the pre-Cana program should be compulsory. They feared that if it were optional, the parents, with traditional attitudes, would discourage young people from preparing themselves in this way.

From these meetings Sister Claire O'Rourke of Providence, Rhode Island, developed an active Family Advisory Center, which concentrates on premarital instruction, family planning, and marriage encounter weekends. Since January of 1974, a laywoman, Mrs. Felisa Tamparong, has been coordinator at the center.

Shortly before leaving Ozamis to begin developing social programs at Davao, on the east coast of Mindanao, Sister Breda earned a nickname. It was given to her by Mr. Siao, an ancient Filipino. She discovered him lying on the bamboo floor of a tiny room, a bent tin mug at his side and a clutter of papers all around. She noticed a dirty bandage wrapped around his left hand and could smell the diseased wound it was covering. He was alone, diabetic, and with a wound already showing signs of gangrene.

After the nun took steps to have the wound cared for Mr. Siao took to hanging around the clinic, making comments in a stilted and mixed English/Chinese/Visayan. One day as he sat watching her work he said quite unexpectedly, "You are humanity." But that wasn't how she got her nickname.

The nickname came when Mr. Siao was confronted by a young nurse who accused him of never following instructions. He grumbled around for the rest of the morning and complained to Sister

Breda that the young nurse is a "wise crow," a title not complimentary in the Philippines.

The expression amused the nun. She repeated it so often in Mr. Siao's presence that it became an "in" joke between them. Then it was that he endowed her with the nickname: Head of the Wise Crows.

23 ✦ From Where
Does the Money Come?

To operate the Archdiocese of Cagayan de Oro, Patrick Cronin has an income from three main sources: the offerings of the people of the archdiocese, the Society of St. Columban, and the Society for the Evangelization of Peoples.

The Society for the Evangelization of Peoples—called the Society for the Propagation of the Faith, before Vatican II—sends the archbishop $7,000 a year, mainly to maintain the seminary, and an additional $5,000 to help with the program of catechetics.

The Society of St. Columban, in addition to providing support for the twenty-five Columban Fathers in the archdiocese, sends the archbishop about $10,000 a year. The society also provides funds annually for projects and programs in aid of the poor, the sick, and the needy.

"The aim is to make the archdiocese self-supporting," said Archbishop Cronin. "This is not easy when a parish priest is doing well if he collects four dollars a Sunday. While he might try to subsist off that, he cannot build a church or a school, finance the catechetics program or buy a jeep and keep it running.

"The Filipino bishops have a greater ability to raise money from among their people than does an outsider. The parishioners know that their own bishops are standing alone and that no one is behind them to lend a hand."

Who are the people standing behind the Columbans of Mindanao lending them a hand? For the most part, they are the friends and supporters of the Columban Fathers in the United States, Ireland, and Australia who generously support their worldwide missionary effort.

Through the magazines published by the Columban fathers, their supporters are kept informed of the work of the missions and often learn of specific needs.

For example, the March 1971 issue of *Columban Mission* ran a story about Hermigildo Erato, a Filipino boy whose leg had been amputated because of gangrene. The readers paid for his trip to Manila where he was fitted with an artificial limb.

"But that doesn't tell the whole story," said Father Michael Cullen. "Columban friends kept sending money for Hermigildo and other poor people in the parish. I decided to use this money as effectively as possible.

"We have many tuberculars in this area and no one to help them. Thanks to the generosity of the readers, fifty tuberculars have been restored to health.

"But these were only stop-gap measures and I decided to start self-help projects in the parish. I bought two sewing machines and borrowed three others from local people, then hired a professional tailor. We now have the nucleus of a free sewing school which has been in operation for several months. So far fifty-two teen-age girls have graduated and twenty-seven others are now enrolled.

"I was also worried about the hundreds of young men in the parish who never go to school and have no hope of any kind of a job. After careful checking I decided to start a *senillas* factory. *Senillas,* cloth slippers, are the usual footwear for the local people and there is always a demand for them. I bought the necessary machine and hired a teacher. We now have a small factory with eleven young men turning out about two dozen slippers a day.

"The boys make about three dollars a week while they are learning this trade. Local housewives help us sell them and they are paid a small commission. So more people are being helped."

What has happened to Hermigildo Erato who started all of this? After a few months in the hospital learning to walk, he returned home without the aid of a cane or crutches. He works in the slipper factory and is adept at operating the sewing machine.

Patrick Cronin is aware that the Columbans have done effective work in Mindanao in spite of a limited budget because they have been helped by some remarkable people. As an example, let's look at the work done by Brother Colman Ryan and Sister Ignatius O'Keefe.

In remote Molave, an area known for the crocodiles in its rivers and the monkeys in its trees, Brother Colman came into Father

Cronin's life. Sister Ignatius came into it a few years later when Patrick Cronin was Bishop of Ozamis.

Upon arriving in the Philippines from China in 1950, Brother Colman's first assignment was to build a high school for Father Cronin in Molave. The quickness with which the new arrival learned things impressed the young Columban. By the time he had finished building the school the brother knew well the timbers of the area and understood local working methods and labor problems. His quickness also led him to such sage observations as "Never say no to a nun. But then you can always forget."

From Molave, Brother Colman went to Tangub to help Father Robert Cullen build a cement church, and from there he moved to Tudela where he began putting together what was to become the celebrated Colman Team. The brother studied each workman carefully and whenever he found one with "star quality" he offered the man a permanent place on his traveling team. Carpenters were easy to come by because up until that time almost all building in Mindanao had been done in lumber. Plasterers, bricklayers, mechanics, electricians, tile-layers, plumbers, and fitters had to be trained, and Brother Colman was the one to do it, for when it came to construction he was truly a Renaissance man.

Under careful tutelage, Doming, the foreman, became another Renaissance man of the building trade. Brother Colman had taken him on as a raw recruit while building the high school for Father Cronin in Molave. Although he had no formal training at any skill, Doming possessed gifts more valuable: a sharp intelligence, an ability to pick up skills quickly, and, above all, character.

Brother Colman preached daily the gospel of good equipment. A builder must have good equipment if he is to cut costs—a recurring theme in his conversation. He proved his point by cutting costs of buildings in half through skillful use of equipment.

As the years went by he picked up all sorts of machines and tools. A large diesel engine supplied power to his motors. He had bench saws, circular saws, and band saws; cement mixers, hoists, and barrows. He was proud of his electric planing machine and electric mortising machine and of his compressors and vibrators, especially of the motors to run this and that machine.

When he moved from one site to another it was a traveling

circus. The children in the *barrios* along the way ran out to watch, bug-eyed, the four trucks loaded to capacity with workmen perched on top. It was a sight to remember!

Upon arriving at a new site the team lost no time. The villagers watched with amazement the speed with which the workshops, storage huts, and sleeping quarters went up. By nightfall everything was in shape. Work began at dawn. From then on, efficiency was the watchword. Work was planned well in advance: for example, windows were made while foundations were being dug. Everybody worked with a wonderful facility.

The men slept at the site and went home for weekends. They had their own cook who bought and prepared the food, well above average in quantity and quality. Their wages, too, were better than that of other men with similar skill and experience. They had the further benefit of security, for their jobs were permanent, with work always waiting for them.

Brother Colman's team completed a job with astonishing speed; six to eight weeks for a rectory, six to eight months for a church. And they were careful "finishers," always rounding off the job neatly and attractively.

Archbishop Cronin said, "Their contribution to our work was invaluable. They cut costs and allowed us to attempt buildings we could not have dreamt of without them. And while they worked away at his church, or new rectory they left the parish priest free to attend to his own special job of ministering to the spiritual needs of his parish."

In his almost twenty years in the Philippines Brother Colman supervised the construction of twelve churches, including the new cathedral of Ozamis, eight schools, a seminary, and six rectories.

Brother Colman became such a legend that when a catechist asked, "Who created the world?" a little boy answered, "Brother Colman." The catechist admitted this was only a slight theological exaggeration considering how many things in the boy's awareness had been created by the brother.

Sister Ignatius O'Keefe was an "old China hand" when she arrived in Bishop Cronin's diocese. Twice she had left the Orient, each time under unfavorable conditions. Her first departure came after she had been carried down from the upcountry mission station desperately ill with typhus. After her long recovery her superiors decided she should work in the United States. Sister Ignatius volunteered to return to China, and did so in 1938, when the Columban sisters asked for nurses trained in pediatrics. She survived World War II, surrounded by Japanese fighting Chinese, only to be expelled by the Communists.

When Sister Ignatius came to Bishop Cronin's diocese to begin a career in teaching she was no longer a young nun. After some years the strain of classroom work began to tell on her voice and another career ended. Of course, she began yet another, that of school nurse.

Many of the children were not sufficiently fluent in English to describe their complaints. Usually a hand placed on the affected spot, and a plaintive *"sakit"* (It hurts here) was all they could manage. Years of looking at children's faces had given Sister Ignatius's eye the penetrating power of an X-ray unit, and years of listening to children's voices had given her ear a nicety of judgment. She could distinguish immediately between the not-so-serious, which she treated, and the serious, which she sent to Dr. Ledesma.

When Father Joseph Shiels needed a nurse for his parish school in Tangub he asked for Sister Ignatius. The elderly nun hurried down and set up a spotlessly clean clinic over which she presided with benignity.

Father Shiels said, "She used to receive large supplies of vitamin tablets from the Catholic Medical Mission Bureau in New York. She distributed them to our children and it made a difference. I can't begin to describe the need for such a supplement to the children's diet. You'd need to do a round of the parish with me to see the homes many of these children come from, to meet them at early morning walking down the mountain to our school, or waiting from six in the morning onwards for a bus that will carry them into town. You'd need to see them arriving home twelve hours later, around sunset, on foot because there is no evening bus to take them.

"You'd need to meet those boys and girls, from twelve to fifteen, who have lodgings in town. They have to do their own cooking and housekeeping. Every Monday morning they bring their modest allotment of rice from home with them, to serve until the next weekend, and a little money for fish and vegetables.

"There was a time when I used to take a stroll through the school during the children's lunch time, but I gave it up. The principal said that it embarrassed my pupils when I was around to see the poverty of the little *balon* they brought with them. If they had merely cold rice they wouldn't feel too ashamed. But often they would have only a couple of boiled bananas, about the equivalent in volume and taste and general attractiveness of one boiled parsnip—cold. And sometimes even this would be gone before lunchtime.

"Well, thanks to the goodness of American Catholics, we had a constant and adequate supply of vitamin tablets. And, thanks to the watchful eye of Sister Ignatius, they reached the children who needed them. I suppose we'll never know just how much good those vitamins did. How much disease was warded off? How much strength and vigor did they bring?"

Sister Ignatius could never be satisfied with one career at a time. While taking care of the children's health she learned that Father Shiels had the burden of seeing to it that between 3,000 and 4,000 children received instruction in catechism.

"Until Sister Ignatius came it was my job to train the volunteer catechists in the fundamentals of teaching catechism," said Father Shiels. "And I supervised their work each week in the classrooms. When Sister offered to relieve me of this duty I gladly handed it over to her. I believed she could do it infinitely better than I could. It gives me great pleasure now to say how right I was.

"She achieved her results by doubling the work of preparation I had demanded from our young catechists—and getting it. Her purpose was to develop in them a painstaking thoroughness which I had thought beyond their capacity and patience, but she, with her deeper understanding, knew what they were capable of.

"The first effect was a marked increase in interest among the catechists themselves. They began to realize their own powers and to enjoy using them. Then they communicated their new enthusiasm to their pupils. What a difference Sister Ignatius made in Tangub! She brought new vitality."

Archbishop Cronin, in speaking of the people who help make

a small Columban budget go a long way, said, "We have to express our gratitude to the different communities of sisters who have worked with us here, and who have been responsible for influencing and moulding the minds and hearts of many of our young people. How impoverished our work would have been without them! When we arrived in Mindanao, the Franciscan Missionaries of Mary already had a school in Oroquieta, which had been opened by a Jesuit. In 1941 the Columban sisters came to Misamis, now called Ozamis, and opened a high school. Unfortunately, the war closed it at Christmas of 1941, and it did not reopen until June of 1945.

"Shortly after the war the Religious of the Virgin Mary—the largest congregation in the Philippines, with more than 700 members—came to Iligan and Plaridel and took over the administration of schools there. These sisters also conduct schools in Gingoog City, Talisayan, and Kinoguitan, parishes under the jurisdiction of the Columbans. The Maryknoll sisters came to Jimenez in 1952. Then the Sisters of St. Paul de Chartres lightened the burden for the priests of Pagadian and Aurora by staffing the schools of those parishes. The Sisters of Mercy of Buffalo have schools in Tubod and Kolambugan, two parishes in Lanao del Norte, and the Irish Sisters of Mercy have taken over the school of Our Lady of Fatima, Mambajao, on the island of Camiguin. The Columban sisters, who now have full college facilities, besides a high school and elementary school in Ozamis City, have expanded their work south to administer schools in Tangub and Molave."

Archbishop Cronin said that while he has no American servicemen in his diocese, they too help the mission budget go a long way. It pleases him to hear of the things they do for the Columbans on the island of Luzon:

In one year United States servicemen donated 12,000 pints of blood to the blood bank in Olongapo. When the crew of the USS Pollux heard that the people of Morong were walking nearly a mile for water, they constructed a dam and laid 3,000 feet of pipeline to the village, all at their own expense. The American Navy wives at Subic Bay helped raise funds to build John XXIII Medical Charity Clinic in Olongapo. A naval doctor and his medical corpsmen helped establish a clinic in San Antonio parish. The crews of the *USS Mount McKinley, USS Saratoga,* and *USS Coral Sea* helped build Boy's Town at Subic Bay.

It's this wide range of people that the archbishop talks about when trying to explain why a certified public accountant is puzzled at how much the Columbans accomplish with their budget. He speaks of nuns, military men, and generous donors as blessings of Providence. He doesn't even want to try to imagine how life would be without them.

24 ✝ Violence of Men

It is not unusual that a priest visiting Archbishop Cronin in Cagayan de Oro brings news of an ambush encountered on the way. Muslim violence in the form of ambushes seems to have grown in intensity in recent years.

The Muslim-Christian conflict sounds as though it might be religious, and yet religion has little to do with it. Roots of the conflict, as Archbishop Cronin explains, are many and deep. More important than theological differences are the struggles for land, food, and living space. Also there are competitions for jobs, wealth, and political power. Incompatible temperaments, ideals, and attitudes cause some of the trouble. Fears of being conquered, bitter memories of past wrongs, and a determination for revenge make the problem more severe than it need be.

To begin to understand the Muslim-Christian conflict we need to look back at least as far as 1900 when Mindanao was almost entirely covered by forests. The population was widely scattered. Moros were mainly in the south, Christians in the north, and pagan tribes in between.

Since the turn of the century, and especially since World War II, Christian immigrants from the overcrowded northern islands have poured into Mindanao to clear and settle great stretches of forests, land classified as government property. The government allows logging rights, and after the trees are felled, it reclassifies the land as agricultural and readily grants legal ownership.

If Muslims living nearby might conceivably lay claim to the land, they are asked to sell and usually do. As far as they are concerned this selling of land is puzzling business; their concept of ownership is so different from that of Christians. The Christian believes in the right of the individual to own land and to buy and sell as he wishes; the Muslim thinks of land as common property of the family or tribe, and, although occupied and used, no one has a lasting claim to it. Since the Muslim sees Christians as land-grabbers he finds nothing wrong with reclaiming and selling the same property several times, which sometimes happens.

The main reason the Muslims did not take part in the opening up of the interior of Mindanao is that they distrust the central government in Manila. They see it as alien to their religion and culture and resent its laws concerning land ownership. All this frustration results in cattle rustling, squatting on other people's property, and murder.

From such conflicts sprung the Mindanao Independence Movement (MIM), a sort of Muslim IRA. Although the MIM represents only a small percentage of the Muslims, it attracts attention with violence and is effective in politics.

During struggles for land, Muslims often use political dexterity to tilt the balance in their favor. Their political skills have been developed through a tradition as traders, visits to Mecca, and, in general, through encounters with the outside world. Such sophistication has sharpened their wits and enabled them to exercise influence in local and national politics out of all proportion to their number, which is about twenty percent in Mindanao.

Christians say that the political power comes more from sharp practices than from sharp wits. The first success the Christians had in pressing these charges came when the supreme court agreed that Muslims had cheated in the elections of 1970.

This legal upset was a factor in the upsurge of violence. Another spur to violence was the declaration of martial law in the Philippines in September of 1972. The law required all citizens to turn in firearms; most Christians did just that, but Muslim guerrillas did not. This advantage encouraged the guerrillas in their violence.

An observer of all this fury is Father Thomas Callanan. He has seen more than his share of outrage since coming to Mindanao with the first Columbans in 1938. Although he knew the suffering and hardship of World War II, he speaks of a day in 1974 as "the saddest and longest day I've ever lived through."

He was awakened by a burst of gunfire shortly after four o'clock in the morning, and as dawn broke, the rattle of machine guns and Garands intensified. The noise came from one of the villages under his care, the village of Kawit Occidental, less than two miles from his parish headquarters in Kauswagan.

"All of us knew what was happening," said Father Callanan. "The Moros had attacked Kawit in a renewed outbreak of the revolt that has plagued these parts for the past three years. We knew there was no way of defending the village. Since martial law was declared the Christians have been disarmed. The Muslims were supposed to be, but it was obvious they weren't. Anyway the shooting continued till about six o'clock when we could see the village was on fire.

"I hurried over there. It was a sight that left me completely numb. I'll never forget. Many of the homes were aflame. A few survivors were coming back to look for the wounded and the dead."

The scenes of anguish were beyond Father Callanan's ability to describe. Children were screaming for their parents. At the first burst of gunfire they had run or crawled into hillside holes or had hid in a nearby swamp. Some fled to the sea to swim to safety along the shore.

Father Callanan counted twenty-two dead.

"The first one I saw was poor Pablo Occeno. His wife was killed and butchered less than two years ago. He lay with a bullet through his brain. Pablo was my leader in the *barrio*. Then I came upon the charred remains of a young man who had graduated from my high school only a few weeks earlier. He and his cousin were slain and their homes burned over them. There was a young mother with a three-day-old baby in her arms. A single bullet had gone through the child's eye and then pierced the mother's heart."

A girl of fourteen led Father Callanan from house to house, searching out the dead and wounded. In several houses he attended the victims while people were still trying to put out the flames. As the girl hurried him along he was weakened by a growing sense of bewilderment and grief.

Violence is also taking its toll in Father Callanan's parish in Kauswagan. The private armies of the Muslims, known as the Barracudas, have killed some seventy of his parishioners. The people who can afford to move do so, returning to the islands from which they came, leaving behind the poor, the refugees, and the pastor.

Considering that some sixty Columbans work in Muslim territory, the miracle is that more of them have not been killed or wounded. Father Martin Dempsey was murdered, as told in the opening pages; Father Donald Kill, of Toledo, Ohio, was seriously wounded.

Father Kill and Father Patrick Reidy were traveling by truck in low gear over a rough road on the way to Aurora. They were taking a sick woman from Tukuran where Muslim insurgents had twice attacked, killing fourteen people.

"About two miles outside of Tukuran we ran into the ambush," said Father Kill. "The first warning was a burst of machine-gun fire which missed us. Then all of them opened fire on us—about ten to twenty firing machine guns and M16s. All of us ducked down as low as possible and as quickly as possible, but I didn't get low enough quick enough. I was hit by one of the first shots. Judging from its path it was a good thing it hit me or it would have hit Pat who was driving. Had he been killed or the truck put out of action that would have been the end of all of us.

"Pat pushed the gas to the floor and since we were in low gear we picked up speed rapidly. It still seemed hours before the shooting stopped. I didn't become unconscious but my right side went into shock and I felt no pain. I looked down and saw red where there used to be a white shirt. I knew immediately I should not look that way again."

Father Kill checked to see how the other six people in the back of the truck had fared. No one else had been hit. Later he learned that Father Reidy had glass and shrapnel in his leg but was not seriously wounded. The sick woman sitting beside him in the cab lost a lock of her hair to a bullet.

"By the time we reached Aurora I was beginning to get dizzy from loss of blood. They stopped the bleeding in the emergency room, then decided I should go by ambulance to Ozamis because there is a better hospital there. In the truck, with thirty bullet holes in it, Pat drove to Ozamis, forty-six miles away, to send an ambulance for me.

"The ambulance arrived five hours later. It turned out to be a long forty-six miles to Ozamis. Because of rough roads it took us three and a half hours and lots of pain. The X rays showed two broken ribs but no internal damage."

Twelve hours later complications developed. What at first appeared as an asthma attack turned out to be an infection in the lung. The doctors were not sure what caused the infection; the only thing evident was that the young priest was not responding to treatment. It was decided to move him to Cebu where there is new equipment, a modern hospital, and expert surgeons.

"It was the right decision," said Father Kill, "even though it was an uncomfortable twelve-hour ferry ride. Four days after I arrived in Cebu the doctors decided that they ought to operate on the right lung which had completely filled with blood and mucus. The operation took over four hours but it cleared up everything. I was soon walking around."

In spite of the horrors described here, the Columban missionaries have made an impressive contribution in Muslim provinces, especially with their high schools. These schools are as accessible to Muslims as they are to Christians. For years Muslims have been delighted to send their children to Catholic schools, which they value highly. In them Muslim beliefs are respected and in no way interfered with. No conversions were ever seriously intended and few resulted. The main object has been to work toward mutual toleration and reconciliation. These good things have come more often than the fanaticism of the guerrilla insurgents would suggest.

When Bishop Cronin sent Father Kenneth Koster to Malabang, in Lanao del Sur in 1955, he said, "You'll be pastor and school director, but temporarily your purpose is not to evangelize the Muslims. You're to establish good relationships with them."

Eighty percent of the children in the school were Muslim but, as Father Koster said twenty years later, he knew of none who had been converted. "Some may have been later in life, but no Muslim is apt to become a Christian before he leaves his native area. If he does he is an outcast for life."

Father Koster realized the wisdom of the bishop's advice when, in time, the Moros went on a rampage and Malabang became a refuge for both Christian and Muslim. The mayor of the town said this was possible because good relationships had become a way of life.

An example of what Columbans are doing to relieve tension showed up in the effort they made after Dimataling was destroyed in April of 1973. The trouble started when a Christian was killed. In retaliation four Muslims were murdered. Then Muslim guerrillas attacked in force again and again. More than fifty people died. Four hundred houses, the Catholic school, and Father Jeremiah Murphy's convent were burned.

Father Murphy and Father Warren Ford went to work putting the town back together again. They established a refugee fund, collected $150,000, and used the money to rebuild homes.

They talked the Christian refugees into returning, but the Muslim refugees took more coaxing. Father Ford said, "We had to get the Muslim refugees back to Dimataling if we were to develop a sense of community and a sense of sharing. We succeeded. But bringing them back was a unique experience.

"The Christians agreed to help the Muslims rebuild their homes. So I left at dawn one morning, crossed the bay and landed at Karomaton, one of our Columban parishes. I had acquired a landing craft for use in this refugee work. First thing was to get rid of a lot of Philippine soldiers who went along with us as security. They were not necessary and I got rid of most of them. We loaded the Muslims aboard the landing craft and took them across the bay to Dimataling. The local government was a bit nervous about the whole operation, but the Muslims were prepared to come with us.

"The craft is licensed to carry thirty-nine people. We counted them as they came off at Dimataling. There were 128 people on board plus baggage. If anything had happened on that trip I was prepared to go down with the ship. It really would have been an embarrassing situation."

Father Ford reported three years later, in March of 1976, that the Muslims had integrated into the community more easily than before the trouble. The 200 families, with their 300 children, have settled in better than the Christians, he believes.

"To rebuild they needed axes, hammers, saws, nails. We loaned them the money, which they repaid quickly. The Muslims are doing their share to improve community relations.

"The Muslim chief built a small cockpit where Christians can come on Sunday and gamble on the fights. Muslims don't gamble. They come and sit around and talk to the Christians. All this helps us demonstrate that Muslims and Christians have nothing to fight about."

Another Columban, Father Martin Noone, said, "The Filipino Muslims are glamorous subjects to writers and photographers. Their dress, customs, and distinctive sailboats in a tropical setting make them picturesque. They are more than that, though. They are a people with a peculiar destiny. They are tormented like so many others by change and upheaval. But most are striving toward a decent and ennobled existence. Those who carry the responsibility of their destiny need to bring with them wise and humane direction."

25 ✛ Violence of Nature

It is not just men who are violent; nature is destructive, too. Patrick Cronin will never forget the night of the earthquake. His car lurched into the dark churchyard, its headlights barely penetrating the clouds of dust. Leaving the lights on, he got out and walked cautiously in the direction he remembered the *convento* to be. Across the rubble the silhouettes of two houseboys and Father Shih drifted toward him.

Suddenly he came upon Father Cornelius Campion sitting on a chunk of concrete examining a deep gash in his left foot. Father Fleming, down on his knees, was trying to stop the blood. Monsignor Cronin quickly helped the injured priest to the car, for it was evident, even in poor light, that he needed a doctor's attention.

It was now 2:45 on the morning of Friday, April 1, 1955. The monsignor had been sleeping in his bed a half mile away when, at 2:20, the earthquake struck with an intensity of eight on the Richter scale. The shock was sufficiently severe so that after a minute and a half many things would never be the same again.

As Monsignor Cronin and Father Campion lurched across the dark, rutted road on the way to the doctor's house they exchanged experiences.

Father Campion said he had awakened to find himself being tossed back and forth with such fierceness that two legs snapped off beneath his bed. The noise made by the rocking of the house was so deafening that he failed to hear the three church bells tolling a few yards away. He looked out the window to see a fog of dust arising around the old Spanish church as one by one the walls collapsed.

He shouted to Fathers Fleming and Shih to get clear of the building. He couldn't take his own advice, however; the door of his bedroom was jammed and a heavy wardrobe had fallen across it. He thought for a moment the quake might cease; instead it gathered force. In desperation he used his fists to beat an opening in the wire mosquito screen that covered the transom above his door. After hauling himself up and through the narrow opening, he jumped down seven feet into the next room and ran down the stairs and out into the open.

The earth quivered, shuddered, and rolled as the three priests and two houseboys knelt down in the debris to say an act of contrition. Upon rising from the ground, Father Campion noticed his left foot was wet and sticky. He paid no attention, thinking it was mud from a burst water system, but soon he felt weak. His foot stiffened and throbbed with such intensity he could scarcely put weight on it. Only then did he realize it had been badly cut in his jump from the transom onto broken glass.

Monsignor Cronin told Father Campion that the procathedral was in ruins. The school buildings next door were badly damaged. The laboratory that the Columban sisters had built up for fifteen years was all gone in a matter of seconds as microscopes, scales, and chemicals were smashed when every cabinet was hurled to the ground.

The sisters were uninjured, except for Mother Eucharia whose foot was badly bruised when a bookcase fell on it. She was being treated when the priests arrived at the doctor's house.

A large wedge of glass was still lodged in Father Campion's foot. After extracting it and closing the wound with steel clips, the doctor explained he had no stitching material because the quake had made the clinic inaccessible.

At 3:30 Fathers Lavin and Fleming arrived at the doctor's house to see if they could be of help. The priests decided to drive around Ozamis; perhaps they might be needed. Of this ride Father Campion wrote a few days later: "We found no serious casualities. Everybody had vacated their houses, preferring to spend the remainder of the night in the street. It was a weird scene that I shall remember for a long time. Here and there horses, terrified by the earthquake, galloped up and down the streets. The cries of frightened children mingled with hymns. The earth still shivered and shook beneath us."

At dawn the priests could see that only a few houses had collapsed, but many were twisted and half fallen. The earthquake seemed not to have moved along any definite path, the buildings leaned in all directions.

Down near the water's edge the city's historical landmark, the 246-year-old Spanish fort, had sunk four feet and was cracked in many places. The lighthouse had sunk five feet and the skulls of Japanese soldiers killed and buried there during the war floated in the sea.

At 5:30 Monsignor Cronin began an open-air Mass at an improvised altar. About 500 people attended. Normally a thousand would have been there because it was First Friday.

Later the Monsignor said: "I can still remember the thoughts that flashed through my mind at Mass—now we have a prelature without a procathedral, a parish of 40,000 without a church.

"I was thankful though that the quake did not wait until 5:30 when there would have been more than a thousand people in the church for the First Friday devotions. God only knows, amidst all the shock and stampede, how many of the thousand would have survived. And how many would have been crippled for life. Had I myself survived in that case I would have blamed myself for delaying construction. I would have been haunted by the thought: If only I had torn down the old building! So I offered a Mass of thanksgiving with a joyful heart on that morning of April 1."

As the day wore on, reports came through from other parts of the island.

In Tangub, where Patrick Cronin had started as a curate, the church was in ruins. And so was the new one he had recently blessed in Bonifacio.

In Kapatagan, Father William Smith told the monsignor, "I got out of bed and headed for the window but was thrown back to the floor. On hands and knees I was approaching the window again when half of it, heavy with glass, flew past me. I jumped from the second story just as the building buckled. Two houseboys were buried in a small space on the ground floor. Not an inch to spare. I got a light and they crawled out unharmed. We lay on the ground away from the house while the tremors still came. The church swayed and I prayed it would not fall. It didn't, but by light of day I found it unsafe."

The worst news Monsignor Cronin heard this day came from

the Lake Lanao area. On that beautiful stretch of shore between Marawi and Malabang, 462 Muslims died in a minute and a half. More deaths resulted from rising waters than from collapsing buildings. The Moros who had built on the shoreline awoke to find their houses slipping into the lake and the waters rising eight feet to engulf them.

When the monsignor learned of the Lake Lanao tragedy he was embarrassed by the discouragement he was beginning to feel. After all, the Columbans and their parishioners had lost only their buildings.

The structures, four churches, four schools, and two *conventos* could be rebuilt. But how? Financially the monsignor and his priests had overextended themselves in that optimistic decade following the war. They had just completed a development program that included building fourteen churches and seventeen schools.

Where would the money come from to cover this financial loss of $250,000, a sizeable sum in the Philippines in 1955? The rebuilding soon began, however, when Pope Pius XII sent $3,000, the Knights of Columbus of America sent $2,500, and President Magsaysay, visiting Ozamis immediately after the quake, personally donated toward the rebuilding of the cathedral.

Although tremors have been usual through the years, the next severe quake did not strike until just after midnight on August 17, 1976. It, too, came with a force of eight on the Richter scale. This time the Columbans suffered less property damage, but the loss of life among their parishioners was high.

A two-story tidal wave caused by the quake thundered down the Moro gulf. When it reached Pagadian on Ilana bay it was no longer a wall of water but a relentlessly rising and boiling tide that smashed everything it engulfed as it swept inland.

The center of devastation and death was a relatively new city built on an incline that sloped gently right out into the bay. Few of Pagadian's residents were born there; most had migrated from the more northern islands of the Philippines hoping for a better future. Many were refugees from troubled areas on Mindanao, areas still plagued by bandits and Muslim rebel bands.

These newcomers lived in thousands of shacks, perched on

stilts, jutting out into the sea. The Columbans visited their parishioners in these jerry-built houses. On many a sick call the missionaries navigated a series of mud and rock dikes, across bridges made of a few boards. These walkways, supported by bamboo stilts driven into the sea bottom, stretched for several hundred yards. Such precarious walkways were connected to the shacks by a single bamboo pole. As one missionary observed, "Though it was a confusing maze it vibrated with life and had a soul of its own, until a boiling surge wiped it out."

One Columban, Father Desmond Hartford said, "As dawn broke, we began to realize the full dimensions of the tragedy. Half of Pagadian was wiped out. We were happy to see the army and civil authorities move right in to start the cleanup operations.

"Later in the day we went around to the funeral parlors and chapels blessing the dead. It was the saddest sight I ever saw in my life. As many as 200 children all lying dead. Many were never claimed because the whole family died in the disaster."

Mothers went to the *funerarias* trying to find their children and hoping they wouldn't. Fathers, searching through the rubble of their shacks to salvage at least a pot or a pan, found the body of a child they thought was safe.

"The courage and resilience of the people was amazing," said a missionary. "I saw one mother almost go beserk when she found her two children laid out side by side in a *funeraria*. She would not be comforted. Yet that afternoon she brought their little coffins to the cathedral to be blessed and the next morning she was hard at work as a volunteer in our social action center passing out food cards."

Another family made three trips to the cathedral with coffins. The father said simply, "Now that we've buried our six children, we'd better go and start rebuilding our home."

The death count quickly rose toward 500. Over 300 were missing—presumably swept out to sea. In the whole province nearly 1,000 died and 36,000 were homeless.

The Columbans have a special interest in earthquakes because most of their work is done in what is known as the Great Pacific Earthquake Belt. The belt runs through the Philippines, Korea,

Japan, Fiji, Chili, and Peru, the countries in which the Columbans have missions.

If "earthquake" is the most dreaded word for them, typhoon is the second most dreaded. After experiencing his first typhoon, Father Michael McShane wrote:

"Suddenly it seemed as if the end of the world had come. The house shook with a deafening roar, swaying to and fro on its poles a number of times, then suddenly stopped as if caught in the arms of a giant angel. The giant angel proved to be a giant tree; we had moved through space about six feet. Though our floor retained a comparatively horizontal position, the walls were inclined at a sharp angle and a portion of the roof had gone.

"All my life I have loved nature in her delicate and her forceful moods, but with a decided leaning toward the latter. I love very high and rough mountains, a mountainous sea smashing itself against a desolate shore, heavy thunders, and a strong wind. But this storm left me cold. Here there was no rapture, no poetry."

Even volcanic eruptions plague Columbans in the Philippines. In Patrick Cronin's archdiocese, on the lush tropical island of Camiguin, stands a majestic killer volcano. Towering above all and belching smoke, Hibokhibok has claimed more than a thousand lives during its three eruptions in living memory. Each time the thunder from it was ear-splitting; balls of fire spurted more than a thousand feet into the air, and hot rocks and lava rained down from the crater bringing black ruin and death to an island resembling Paradise.

The missionaries observe that no matter how nature lashes out —with earthquake, typhoon, or volcanic eruption—they rarely hear a word of bitterness from any parishioner. As one Columban said, "The Filipino says, 'Pagbuat Sa Dios'. It is the will of God. This is no fatalistic acceptance. It means, God knows best; I don't understand, but I trust him."

Patrick Cronin has tried to learn resignation from the Filipinos. When he sees things destroyed through the violence of men or of nature he says, "Pagbuat Sa Dios". Such trust comes more readily with age, at least it does for him.

26 ✣ Unrest in the Philippines

A rchbishop Cronin still remembers with regret the dawn of
Saint Patrick's Day in 1957. He awoke to hear the news-
caster sob as he announced that the burned body of President
Magsaysay had been found in the mountain jungles of Cebu Island
in a charred Dakota.

Raymon Magsaysay, tall and broadly built, had given extraordinary service to the Filipinos. He was their hero, their friend, the
guardian of their rights. He had appeared on the scene as a fighter
against Japanese invaders in December of 1941. After the collapse
of American defenses, he continued as a guerrilla leader in his
native province of Zambales, preparing the way for MacArthur's
return in 1945. The following year he was elected to the Philippine
Congress.

In 1950, as defense secretary, he began a successful fight against
Communism by reorganizing and disciplining the Philippine army
and sending it against 20,000 Huks. Those dissidents, led by Communists, had terrorized the countryside, infiltrated the government, and were planning to seize Manila.

At the time Magsaysay began his campaign, a Columban was
taken prisoner by the Huks. On the night of October 30, 1950,
Father Thomas Flynn was led from his presbytery in Laborador,
northern Luzon, by raiding guerrillas and never seen again. He is
presumed to have been killed by them, possibly in a nearby store
where some bones thought to be his were discovered.

Magsaysay's personal leadership in the front lines in those uneasy days so boosted the army's morale that within two years he
had eliminated any serious threat of domination by Communists,
at least for the time being. Then he struck psychologically, offering
"all-out force or all-out fellowship." Some Huks went down
fighting, some went to prison, but many accepted land and settled
down to a new life in the cleared forest areas of Mindanao.

Magsaysay had the knack of making things work, observed

Archbishop Cronin. His policy toward the Huks was especially successful. Perhaps the best way to explain this is to look at what happened in one *barrio,* Buriasan.

When Father Terence Twohig was pastor of Kapatagan he used to visit Buriasan, a mission station ten miles away. From the very beginning he was impressed with the spirit of unity and cooperation found there. In trying to discern what made that *barrio* work so well he talked to one of the early settlers, Lieutenant Abecia.

"Father, when I came here in 1951 this place was still a jungle," said Abecia. "No motor vehicle could reach Buriasan; you walked or rode a horse or you didn't get here. Wild life was abundant in the forest—wild pigs, monkeys, snakes, and birds. Here and there was a small clearing. A few Muslim homes and one or two Christians. Hardy pioneers. It might still be like that except for Raymon Magsaysay."

Magsaysay had chosen this backwoods jungle, hemmed in by mountains and hills, as one of the areas for the Huks to settle. He ordered the engineers to build a fine road into the valley so that the ex-rebels, mainly farmers, could bring in their families. He was realistic enough to send in a military unit to make sure everything went well; with this unit came doctors, dentists, and even a Catholic chaplain.

During the early years it was hard going. Even though the Misamis Lumber Company felled and hauled away the heavier trees, the jungle undergrowth and brushwood had to be cleared away and kept from returning to smother the crops. Although each farmer got a *carabao,* a horse, a plow, seeds, plants, and fertilizers to start with, he had to contend with the wild pigs, snakes, and monkeys which destroyed much of the corn and vegetables. Crocodiles played havoc with any pigs or chickens meandering too near the spawning ground.

Some of the first settlers gave up the struggle, but most persevered against great odds. Hardship fosters good spirit, said Lieutenant Abecia. He told of the way the community had built a village for some ex-Huk settlers who were being harassed by bandits in remote areas.

"Buriasan is now on its feet," said the lieutenant. "We have a cooperative. We've developed coconut groves. We're replacing nipa huts with bungalows made of concrete blocks. We have a population of 6,000, and three elementary schools with about 400 pupils in each. Now we want a high school. We're ready to spread our wings and fly."

An ex-Huk soldier, Juan de la Cruz, told Father Twohig that he still thinks he was justified in continuing to struggle after the war. He felt justified until "The Big Fellow," as Magsaysay was called, gave him a helping hand.

Archbishop Cronin believes that it was Magsaysay's amazing success in handling the Huk revolt that made him an obvious choice for the presidency. In November of 1953 the nation rewarded him by sending him, at age forty-six, to the presidential palace with an unprecedented two-to-one majority. Immediately, he summed up his feelings about power when he admonished his cabinet: "One thing I want you to remember. You must pay attention to the little fellow. The big people always manage to take care of themselves."

Since Patrick Cronin was interested in developing a school system he felt a special loss in the deaths of two men who went down in the plane with President Magsaysay. Both Gregorio Hernandez and Jesus Peredes had been helpful to the Columbans and other missionaries.

Until Hernandez was appointed by Magsaysay as secretary of education, an abundance of red tape made difficult all efforts to provide religious education in the schools. After Hernandez took office he reviewed the regulations concerning religious education and simplified them.

Paredes, an able lawyer, helped the work of the Church by organizing the Catholic Education Association. This organization helped raise the quality of parish schools.

On that sad St. Patrick's Day of 1957, Patrick Cronin wondered if the Huks would rise again. They did, a decade later, in four provinces in Central Luzon, but not in Mindanao. The new Huks were different from the old. They lacked political and military leadership and did not seem inspired by Communism. They were more of a law-and-order problem than a political one.

Just when the Huk movement was being reborn a National Congress for Rural Development was held. In his opening address, President Marcos admitted "We are standing on a volcano. We have no more time to lose."

He observed that of the thirty-three million people only about one percent enjoys an income of $4,000 or more a year. About seventy percent must make do with less than a hundred dollars a year.

Marcos said, with feeling, that it is time for religious and political leaders to work together for rural reconstruction and urban renewal. He closed his talk by proclaiming the period from May 1, 1968, to April 30, 1969, as Social Action Year.

The bishops responded to this plea by urging all Christians to cooperate in the government's land reform program. They asked priests and nuns and lay people to set an example by sponsoring credit unions, cooperatives, and technical, vocational, and agricultural training programs.

About this time, in 1967, Jeremias Montemayor, resigned his position as dean of the law school at the Ateneo, the Jesuit university in Manila, to start a social program. He founded and became president of the Federation of Free Farmers, a national organization of farmers, tenants, and small landowners.

Although Pope Paul VI appointed Montemayor a consultor to the Council of the Laity, a department of the Holy See, some Church authorities were suspicious of the Federation of Free Farmers and its president.

"For a time" said Montemayor, "they viewed us with suspicion and some animosity. They thought we were troublemakers and some even suspected that we were Communists. But this attitude has changed. They believe now that we are real Christians working for social justice, that we are trying to implement the social teachings of the Catholic Church. So more and more bishops are inviting us these days to give seminars to their clergy. And after we do that the whole diocese supports the movement; so, in many areas of the Philippines we are now undergoing rapid expansion."

As for the politicians, Montemayor described them as "very flexible people." He said they help when it is politically expedient and oppose when it is politically necessary.

Montemayor was an enigma as far as the Communists were concerned. They couldn't understand why he was not immedi-

ately accepted by the bishops, for his statements always under-
lined spiritual and moral values.

"I believe that never did they doubt the fact that I was not a
Communist," said Montemayor. "I don't think they were ever
deceived on this point. They may have doubted my position in the
Church."

Montemayor explained that he is organizing the farmers all
over the Philippines to generate sociopolitical power to defend
their rights against anyone who would exploit them. "We help
them file the proper cases in court so that they will get a just share
of the harvest, and so they will not be ejected from the land for
flimsy reasons. For some, we help them acquire title to land for
which they have been working and applying under our land laws."

To be more definite about this, perhaps it would be well to tell
of the plight of the farmer as seen by one Columban, Father
Robert Burke. In his parish of 16,000 souls there are more than
500 small farmers. Most live in an atmosphere of hardship and
numbing insecurity. The tenant farmer's lot is even worse, for he
tills soil not his own. After twenty years of back-breaking labor
he will probably have nothing more to show for his work than the
clothes on his back. His meager wages go for clothes and medicine. When he gets sick he is sent away, for he is of no further use
to the landowner. This situation in one Columban's parish could
be multiplied a thousand times throughout the Philippines.

At the opening of Social Action Year, in May of 1968, Father
Burke started the Farmers Cooperative. He selected forty-four
farmers and educated them in the spirit and workings of a cooperative. In less than a year the members were finding a new confidence in themselves and in their church. So many farmers wanted
to join the organization that Father Burke wrote to the Agricultural Development Foundation in Manila asking for help.

The Agricultural Development Foundation was started by Cardinal Rufino Santos to help needy areas. He placed at the head of
the foundation Father Francis Sendin, CICM, a respected sociolo-
gist. In a short time the priest enlisted the cooperation of leading
sociologists, economists, and agricultural experts.

The government of President Marcos is so impressed with
the federation that when the organization, after a careful sur-

vey of a critical area, asks for funds it usually gets them. For example, when the ADF received an immediate reply from a credit agency in the form of a 400,000-pesos loan for a major agricultural project, and someone objected, Governor Valley, the director, replied, "The signature of the priest is sufficient guarantee for me."

When Father Burke asked for help the Agricultural Development Foundation sent two technical experts to his parish—Dr. Bart Lapuz, a specialist in agriculture, and Mr. Gill Arriola, an economist. After traveling about the parish examining local methods of farming, storage, transportation and marketing they said that their findings were shocking. For instance, only one farmer in the whole area had ever obtained a soil analysis of his land. The lack of know-how had resulted in overfertilization on some farms, insufficient pest control on others, and hit-and-miss methods throughout the area.

One of the farmers interviewed was Vincente Gohel, owner of six acres. Because he was a typical farmer of the area, he was used as a guinea pig. The experts studied his methods, pointed out the problems and suggested solutions while all of his neighbors looked on.

The rice crop on Vincente's farm was of poorer quality than it needed to be. Dr. Lapuz recommended a different variety of seed, one that needed only four months to come to harvest compared with the six months of the old seed. With better timing of planting periods and improved irrigation, his neighbors saw Vincente produce three times as much rice as usual, plus an additional crop of corn.

This brought him about five times his former profit with only a little additional expense. Vincente and his neighbors couldn't believe their eyes. A whole new world was opening before them. But more was to come.

Mr. Arriola, the economist, explained how the marketing of Vincente's product could be protected by a cooperative. Now instead of being the victim of unscrupulous buyers from the capital who underweigh and undervalue his produce at harvest time, Vincente could store his rice in the warehouse of the cooperative and wait for more favorable market conditions. Storage, bulk selling, transportation, and marketing were new words that opened new worlds to the semi-illiterate farmer.

Mr. Arriola and Dr. Lapuz believe that, since agriculture is the basis of the Philippine economy, the place to start uplifting the people is on the farms. They feel that the volcano President Marcos spoke of will have to be cooled down in many ways and that the most important way to cool it is to improve life on the land.

27 ✚ Martial Law

A rchbishop Cronin said, "Martial law was a temporary necessity that could have a long-range disastrous effect. I trust President Marcos, but who will come after him? Some strong-armed general? If kept too long, martial law might destroy democracy. In the summer of 1977 President Marcos said that he will end martial law in a year; if he does, that will be to his credit."

An outsider is aware of the situation as soon as he reaches an airport. Sometimes there are as many as three baggage checks, a body search, and a demand for identification papers. Soldiers encircle the plane with automatic rifles at the ready. This is how it has been since September 21, 1972, the day Marcos declared martial law.

At the time, most citizens agreed that such an action was necessary if the republic was to survive. Starting in the 1960s the government's authority was seriously challenged, mainly by students urged on by radical groups. The Communist Party, with its military arm, the New People's Army (NPA), and the Muslim secessionists in Mindanao and in Sulu were powerful forces to be reckoned with.

President Marcos said he committed almost fifty percent of his armed forces and organized several task forces to try to cope with the challenge, but still could not contain the violence. "In 1969," he said, "the NPA conducted raids, resorted to kidnapings, and took part in other violent incidents numbering over 230, while inflicting 404 casualties. Things degenerated until our economy came to a stop. The country was in a state of anarchy."

An international commission of jurists studied the years of martial law, and in August of 1977 described the conditions that prevailed: "During this period Parliament and all political activities have been suspended, and severe restrictions have been imposed on virtually all basic human rights and fundamental freedoms, including freedom of speech, expression, association, and assembly, freedom of the press, freedom from arbitrary arrest, from prolonged detention without trial, and from torture and ill-treatment, the right to speedy public trial, the right to strike, and the right of the people to choose their own government."

The Church is divided in the matter of martial law. Of the seventy-five bishops in the Philippines a small group supports Marcos's policy, believing it is best under the trying circumstances. Another small group is decidedly against the present government and urges opposition with every means short of violence. The attitude of the majority is one of critical temporary acceptance, meaning that while accepting the temporary necessity for martial law they retain their right to criticize the government and its policies.

When interviewed by the Foreign Correspondents Association of the Philippines Cardinal Sin of Manila said he was deeply concerned about the indefinite detention of political prisoners. Some have been confined for more than two years without charges and without the prospect of an early trial.

"I would like the government to issue a clear-cut definition of what subversion is," said Cardinal Sin. "Right now it is a catchall term that could include almost anything and everything. The government should clarify the question if it hopes to eliminate the creeping climate of fear and uncertainty that is threatening the country."

The Association of Major Religious Superiors of the Philippines, in cooperation with the government, has set up a task force to help detainees. Members of the task force go into prisons to minister in every possible way. The operation does not always run smoothly. When some nuns were accused of smuggling prohibited items into the stockade they insisted on being searched each time they entered.

Cardinal Sin said that Church-military liaison groups have been organized to consider cases of injustice and to help gain an early release of detainees against whom no charges have been filed. These groups, the Cardinal said, have achieved a fair measure of success.

"I commend the efforts of the leaders of the armed forces to curb abuses. I am afraid, however, that they have not been altogether successful. I know of cases of torture and brutal killings which have happened and which the Church has protested against. I have well-documented reports of these cases."

Archbishop Cronin was one of fourteen members of the Filipino hierarchy who made objections to the torture of Mrs. Trinidad Herrera, president of an organization that numbers 20,000 slum dwellers. The archbishop said, "I think it can be very truthfully stated that certain prisoners were tortured. However, I think we can accept the statement of the president that 'it is not the policy of the government to torture anyone, and those who use this weapon of torture will be punished.'"

In the December 1975 issue of the magazine *Missi,* Paul Brunner, a journalist, said that when martial law was proclaimed in 1972 the Church as a whole accepted it with relief, seeing it as a way of ending political and economic chaos. But there is an active minority among the clergy, and especially among the sisters, who do not hide their opposition to the Marcos regime. Brunner observed that the dissenters at that time could count on the support of about five bishops and the Association of Religious Superiors. "This group demands an immediate return to democratic liberties. That is an illusion."

Commenting on Brunner's statement, Archbishop Cronin said that many of the bishops now wish for a peaceful and almost immediate return of democracy with all its faults. But there are still many others who have confidence in Marcos and are satisfied with the steps he is now taking toward a return to democracy.

Father Thomas Callanan said, "When we go to Marcos to tell him of an injustice—and if we are sure of our ground—he takes action." Yet Father Callanan has found some aspects of martial law frustrating. "It has disarmed all the Christians but failed to disarm any Muslims here in Lanao del Norte. The armed forces who are sent to protect the people are inadequate in number and arms. They are fine enough men but what can they do without the necessary power."

He was talking about the murder of six young men, his neighbors in Kauswagan. On September 22, 1975, just as the youths reached their farm outside of town they were ambushed by Muslims, first shot and then butchered. "What a sad day it was as their bodies were brought home in that awful condition to their grieving parents. It would touch a heart of stone to see the first one brought in. He lived in a house, or shack, too poor and fragile to wake his body. It would collapse if many people entered. A good neighbor provided his own home for the purpose. The boy of fourteen lay there with his hands folded over his mutilated and bloody figure. On his hand was one of those tiny red rubber bands. It was his worldly wealth.

"These killings happen all the time. Scarcely a week goes by that somebody is not either wounded or killed. Today the poor families are frantically trying to provide enough wood and nails to make coffins."

President Marcos does not take clerical pressure lying down. In late 1976 his government deported two American missionaries, closed two Catholic publications, *The Sign of the Times* and *The Communicator,* and arrested more than a hundred Christian workers. This had to be done, the president explained, because the stability of the government is being threatened by the Christian left.

Marcos says that, as the voting shows, his policy has the overwhelming approval of Filipinos. The people voted in January of 1973 to ratify the new constitution; the following July they agreed that Marcos should continue in the presidency; in December of 1973 and in February of 1975 they voted to continue with martial law. In January of 1976 the referendum resulted in a constitutional amendment authorizing the president to rule by decree.

Marcos's critics say the votes give a false impression because they were cast while martial law was in effect and opposition leaders were either in jail or living in fear of prosecution. Press, radio, and television were being censored. The polling was done with soldiers patrolling the voting booths.

The international commission of jurists reported, in August of 1977, that they feel martial law is no longer necessary. It is kept in force "to perpetuate the personal power of the president and his collaborators and to increase the power of the military to control Philippine society." (Marcos was elected president in 1965 and reelected in 1969. Under the constitution no person shall serve as president for more than eight consecutive years. So his term of office would have expired on December 30, 1973.)

Opponents of Marcos hold against him more than his policy of martial law. They say that although he has broken up some oligarchies and has promised to build a new society with opportunities for all, he is really replacing one feudal order with another. They point out that he has appointed his wife, Imelda, governor of Metro Manila and that his relatives sit in high places on corporate boards and in government agencies. Imelda's uncle, Eduardo Romualdez, is the Philippine ambassador to Washington. Marcos's sister is governor of Ilocos Norte, his home province. A relative is secretary of education. His brother is chairman of the Medicare Commission. The four English-language newspapers in the Philippines, and the radio and television stations are said to be in the control of the Marcos and Romualdez families, their aides, or their friends.

This gave rise to the joke: Today everything in politics is relative. If you're not one you don't have a chance.

28 ✛ Changing Ways

Just as there is a generation gap within families, in academia, and in the arts, there is one to be found among missionaries all over the world. The priorities of Patrick Cronin's generation are not always those of the younger generation.

Fortunately, the archbishop has been able to bridge the gap. He has been able to do this, said the superior general of the Columbans, the Very Rev. Anthony O'Brien, because he embodies an attitude that Paul expressed to the Corinthians:

"There is a variety of gifts but always the same Spirit. There are all sorts of services to be done, but always to the same Lord. Working in all sorts of different ways in different people, it is the same God who is working in all of them. The particular way in which the Spirit is given to each person is for a good purpose."

Patrick Cronin's generation were pioneers, builders of churches and schools, but the tendency now is to spend more money on social action programs, for the young missionaries want to see the good things of God's world better distributed. The older men stressed the need for vocations, while the younger ones are concerned with developing a priesthood of laymen. The pioneer poured into his parishioners what he had brought with him; the new missionaries say they seek enrichment from the goodness found in their people. The early missionaries approached other religions as competitors, but the younger ones stress the value of all religions, searching out the inspiration in each.

These shifts in attitude were much discussed at a conference of Asian bishops, priests, religious, and laity held in Hong Kong in the spring of 1977. They said, for example, that one of of the Church's problems is learning "how to enrich its Christian identity and life by opening itself to the great religious traditions of Asia." They believe the Church will have to become allied with other religions in a fight against atheism; it will need to become really "catholic" by introducing into its life the riches of all nations.

Missionaries realize that the Church should not just teach; it should learn too. Many are learning to enrich their own lives within their own religion by drawing inspiration from the spiritual experiences of those in other religions. The time is right for this.

Cardinal Bea, when head of the Vatican Secretariate for Christian Unity, said in January of 1964, "The Counter Reformation is over." It had been a long siege, four hundred years of militancy, rigor, and uniformity, characteristics of any organization that is attacking or counterattacking. Now the period is past when the Roman Catholic Church is conditioned to react to Protestantism.

Since Vatican II, the Christian Churches sense that the advancement of one is the advancement of all. They no longer feel that ground can be gained on one front at the expense of another. There is a suggestion that all religions may come to realize that they advance together or diminish, a feeling that they might need all the unity they can get when the believers in God are confronted by those who say there is no God.

Father Walbert Bühlman, a Swiss priest with years of experience in the missions, said, "When we do come to the baptism of an individual, this should not entail a final break in his loyalty to his social, cultural, and religious past. As Hinduism is, in the first place, a form of social community and leaves plenty of room in matters of faith, we could in the future think of 'Catholic Hindus.' These would be persons, or preferably whole families, who have become Christian but continue to celebrate Hindu rites, interpreting them in a new way and receiving Christian sacraments in addition. . . . just as the apostles continued to attend the synagogue and celebrated the Eucharist in addition."

At the meeting in Hong Kong the conference stressed that the Church must do its best to help solve social questions. The more a missionary tries this the more he is apt to become involved in political conflict. It is here that the gap between the generations is probably the greatest. The pioneers tend to agree with the attitude that Father John La Farge, S.J., expressed in his autobiography, *The Manner is Ordinary:* "It is difficult to know which is

more disastrous in the long run, the meddling of ecclesiastics in the affairs of the country beyond their actual competence, or the meddling of the State in Church affairs, which is very apt to be the result of the former. A vicious circle is set up with disastrous consequences for all."

One of the first signs of the missionary's new concern with politics came in a document issued by the bishops of Madagascar in 1953. When the French army had just put down a rising for independence, the bishops said in their Christmas message that political freedom is part of the basic human rights and that the Church recognizes self-government as a natural right.

The key word in that last sentence is *self*. The emerging nations want to govern themselves, and individuals, too, are painfully self-aware. As former colonials they now want to make their presence felt in the world. They are no longer satisfied to sit in the shade of western civilization, but keep surging forward shouting, "Look at me!"

The Christian communities as much as the secular states cry out, "Let us be ourselves!" They are no longer willing to accept an imposed system, no longer willing to "live by the book." This is what missionaries mean when they use the awkward word, *indigenization*.

"An appreciation of our own uniqueness and worth has grown considerably in the past few years," said a missionary sister in Hong Kong. "We are less satisfied than formerly to take over wholesale a project, book, or program from another country. We easily label ideas from other places 'not for us.' This is partly our own brand of nationalism rearing its head. But it has thrown us on our own resources, brought out talents we did not know existed, forced us into projects we once thought impossible."

Another awkward word, *inculturation*, is used by some missionaries. To describe its meaning, Father Catalino Arevalo, S.J., in a talk to Columbans in the Philippines, used the analogy of a young person moving toward maturity, on the way to developing full selfhood. "He must interiorize, personalize, make truly his own, whatever has been learned and experienced in the past, from parents and others. Then all this must be assumed into a project of the creation of one's own selfhood, one's own personal identity.

In this the assumption is that each person has a set of gifts, a pattern of selfhood that is his own, not quite the same as that of anyone else.

"Similarly each people has a set of gifts, a pattern of selfhood as a people that is not quite the same as any other people's. The growth toward that selfhood is the creation of a truly original history and identity. The embodiment of this, within the Christian life and the Christian reality, is what the process of incarnation/inculturation tends toward, a new people with its own gifts, its own original contribution, to the whole people of God."

Adaptation used to be a word much used in missionary countries, but now the time for adaptation is past. The African bishops, in their Mission Sunday statement in 1974, condemned the theology of adaptation. They said it was tied to colonialism and so is entirely unacceptable today. Three years later the Asian conference said that instead of bringing in a culture, the Church must help develop the culture that is there. It is no longer a matter of tutelage, of implanting western ways, but of helping the emerging nations to flower in their own good way. The Church should not be "foreign" in its religious expression, symbolism, or organization. Not even the Gospels will for long be preached merely in "translation" but will be seen from a new angle of vision. "Asian churches," said the conference "must become truly Asian in all things."

Since Archbishop Cronin believes that there is a plan in the history of salvation, he feels optimistic even when there appears to be a crisis in the Church. He once wrote to his superior general that he has been reading about the Middle Ages and finds consolation in learning that the Church then had problems as great as those of today.

He senses that through inculturation the Church, for the first time in its history, will become a Church of all peoples instead of a Church saturated by European culture. He sees the spirit of a people on the move as giving an infusion of energy and inspiration. This could bring new vitality to the tired Church of the West.

29 ✛ Christian Kibbutz

Patrick Cronin's way of looking at things helps him accept the changing world of the missionary. For one thing he is willing to admit that yesterday's solutions are not necessarily effective in solving today's problems. He also enjoys enough optimism to prefer thinking of opportunities offered the Church rather than focusing on the crisis of the Church.

So he was pleased that the Asian conference held in Hong Kong in the spring of 1977, and the World Synod of Bishops, meeting six months later in the Vatican, spoke a great deal about the evolving concept of basic Christian communities. The bishops said that such communities could be formed by occupation—say fishing, or by interest—such as education, or by age—perhaps the elderly. The only requirement of the endless possibilities, the bishops agreed, is that these communities lead to a fuller participation in Christian living. "These groups are not the only way of participating in the life of the Church, still the Spirit seems to be moving the Church strongly in this direction."

Karl Rahner, the theologian, said, "The Church of the future will be built up from below through basic communities of free initiative and free association. We should do our best not to put obstacles in the way of such development but to promote it and guide it along the right lines."

The idea for such basic groups was developed at a Latin American bishops' conference at Medellín in 1968. The idea took root and apparently thrived. According to Father Walbert Bühlmann in *The Coming of the Third Church* (Orbis Books, 1977; p. 257)

The Church in Latin America no longer consists only of sumptuously adorned cathedrals and places of pilgrimage visited by the masses: it consists also of committed young Christians who make a decisive contribution to progress, of peasants who preach the gospel, of family men who sacrifice their free time for the community. Here and there, the Churches are full again on Sundays; people who, until yesterday, only prayed to St Anthony, St Philomena or St Wendelin, now gather to meditate together on the Bible. The spirit of Medellín has been given concrete expression in documents from bishops, priests and groups of lay people; these have gone very far and could be used as models on the other sides of the Atlantic and Pacific. They show how a local church has become aware of itself after centuries of dependence and has found its own solutions. The experiments and pastoral experience of Latin America are more significant than the theology of liberation and can, with better reason, be taken as the contributions offered by the continent to the universal Church.

An example of a basic Christian community formed in the Philippines is that started by a young Columban, Father Niall O'Brien, several years before the Asian bishops or the World Synod presented their reports. He conceived the idea and decided to act on it after being pushed to the decision by a series of painful experiences.

One such experience began late at night with a knock on the door. Nanding, a laborer at the *hacienda,* said that Clarita, his wife, was about to give birth. Would the priest drive her to the hospital?

When twin girls were born prematurely Father O'Brien baptized Margarita and Banilda immediately. The infants had to take turns at the oxygen because the hospital, run commercially by the local sugar mill, had a makeshift incubator that could care for only one baby at a time.

"Nanding had brought with him a small tin of the cheapest milk," said Father O'Brien. "It was the best he could afford. I thought I'd surprise them and send over a big tin of the best milk. By then Margarita was dead. Banilda died the next day. The milk went untouched.

"I said nothing. But I kept wondering what sort of economic system produced wealthy sugar mills which couldn't get around to buying a simple incubator. There's money in sugar, but the workers don't benefit from it. I had happened to see the account books of one of the *haciendas.* It was a pretty decent plantation with an owner more enlightened than most. He was making $100,000 a year, but only about $10,000 was going to the total labor force of sixty families. I thought to myself, 'If I were running this farm I could pay the workers a decent wage and still make money.' "

When Father O'Brien went to Nanding's house at the edge of a large sugar cane field he found a nipa roof and matted walls full of holes. The missionary thought to himself that he wouldn't even put a car in there, not if he wanted to shelter it from sun and rain.

Nanding was alone, for Clarita was still at the hospital. The young father led the priest to where Margarita and Benilda were laid out in pink dresses on top of a wooden box. As the priest knelt to pray he noticed it wasn't dresses they were wearing but pink crepe paper. Then he and Nanding sat on the floor, for the house had no table or chair.

"Father," said Nanding, "we have a problem. Some say we should bury them in one coffin and some say in two. What do you think?"

"What do you think yourself?"

"I think they should be buried in two coffins in two holes."

"Why?"

"Because they are two."

In recalling the conversation, Father O'Brien said, "The answer thrilled me. It thrilled me to think that in the midst of all this sorrow and poverty Nanding's understanding of the dignity of the human being was far above what our shining society had taught him."

Father O'Brien asked Nanding if he would like to attend a Mass at dawn, but the young father declared, "No, I'm afraid the *aswang* (bad fairy) will take the children. Do you believe in the *aswang,* Father?"

The Columban felt that if he said, "No" he would be wrong. "I now believe that life is larger than logic. We missioners have often exorcised the demons from a people only to find that what we had exorcised was some precious cultural value. I'm inclined to be slow with condemnations of this kind. And I felt that to say 'No' was to put my superior education against his. It would be like saying, 'Your children died because you're poor and you are poor because you believe such nonsense.' "

So Father O'Brien cupped Nanding's hands in his own and said, "I don't know what I believe about this. But I do believe in your love for your children because you will stay up all night watching them."

Nanding watched the dead babies until dawn. At the burial Father O'Brien blessed separate coffins just before they were lowered into separate graves.

The priest went to the hospital that evening to see Clarita. She held his hand and said, "Father, it is painful. Don't go away." He noticed that the dextrose had stopped flowing and asked the nurse if a doctor could be contacted. The doctor wrote some prescriptions and gave them to Nanding, who hurried off.

"Where's he going?" asked the priest. "Isn't there medicine in the hospital?"

"No," the nurse said. "If we kept medicines here we'd never be paid for them. He's gone back to the *hacienda* to get the administrator to sign the prescription; then he'll bring it to the *botica* (pharmacy) and wake them up and get the medicine."

"That'll take two hours!" said Father O'Brien as he hurried after Nanding. He signed the prescription and sent a messenger to the *botica.* The medicine did not ease Clarita's pain so the priest asked the doctor for some other medicine and ran to the pharmacy with the prescription.

Clarita's womb had been ruptured with the twins. The doctor said he would operate in the morning. Nanding and the priest sat on the bed, each holding one of Clarita's hands.

"Father," she said, "if I die, please give advice to Nanding whenever he needs it."

Nanding's tears began to fall on her. "Don't worry," she said.

At one o'clock she took off her ring and asked Nanding to wear it. At two o'clock she died.

Clarita was laid out in the hospital morgue with a five-centavo piece on each eye to keep them closed. It was then Father O'Brien cried without shame.

Such incidents built up inside the Columban for a dozen years. He suffered each time he watched his parishioners in the cane fields—a miserable job, backbreaking, hot, suffocating—for less than a dollar a day and only six months of work a year. If only he could think of a way to improve their lives!

He dreamed of starting a community farm where the workers would share in the profits. He didn't have much hope, though. Such a farm would cost more money than he was ever apt to see.

One day his dream came true. A friend in the United States sent him $10,000. His elation was somewhat dampened, though, when he found himself facing a problem unforeseen—landowners refused to sell. When they heard that the missionary wanted to put laborers in charge of the farm it went against all they believed.

Finally, in the distant mountains, Father O'Brien was able to buy twenty-five acres. It was poor land, but it would have to do. One day in 1973 he told the first four men selected for the project that it was time to go. He paid off their debts and bought clothes, cane knives, and a *carabao* plow. Then off they went to Tall Grass Mountain, leaving their families behind until they could provide housing for them.

"I started off with the idea of an honestly run farm," said Father O'Brien. "Then a cooperatively run farm. Then a communally run farm. It was only after we were already going that I realized what we had was a *kibbutz.* I got interested and began to read up on the kibbutz in Israel and Tanzania and wrote for information from both countries."

Ten families are on the kibbutz now. They have separate dwellings but share a common house for meals and recreation. The members administer the farm themselves, control all the money and participate in all decisions.

Everybody works and no outsiders are hired. The men handle the field work and repair the homes. Women cook, sew, weave, and take turns minding the twenty children. Even the children have jobs. When not in school they work in the fields and take care of the *carabao.*

Fortunately, the kibbutz is located near a cooperative sugar mill sponsored by the local bishop. At the mill the kibbutz members have the reputation of producing the cleanest cane and highest yield.

In the first year of operation the new community cleared nearly

$10,000. Each family took a salary of $500 and the rest went to pay debts, buy equipment and expand. Six more acres were added, allowing twenty-nine acres for cane and two for vegetables.

Father O'Brien visits the community twice a month. He said, "This is no panacea for all sugar workers. I only hope it shows how the *hacienda* system should be run. No matter how high the wages are on a sugar farm, the work is hell if not humanized. The day you own the cane that you're cutting, that's the day you begin to enjoy your work.

"As Christians our vocation is to spread Christ's message of love. You can do it with sermons, but when people are living in a society whose structures militate against loving, it is hard for love to flower. Perhaps this alternative structure will show more and more that there can be a way of life in which to love one another becomes easier. Unlike Communism, which went wrong in its rejection of God, the basis of the kibbutz is to share everything because of God."

The angelus and the rosary are regular practices in the kibbutz. Here husband and wife together are receiving theoretical and practical instruction in religious and secular matters. Chances are this will lead to the development of more complete individuals blessed with self-regard and dignity. In this hope Father O'Brien named his new community *Iwag Santa Maria,* "Beacon of Our Lady."

30 ✛ Patience with the People

Although Patrick Cronin is in sympathy with many of the changes, he does not find the new code words springing readily to the tongue. Such words as indigenization, inculturation, ministeriality, charisms, and conscientize are alien to his vocabulary. He is still capable of using such an old-fashioned word as patience.

The advice he gives concerning patience is much the same as the old Archbishop of Manila, Michael J. O'Doherty, used to give. He would point to a *carabao* lumbering along, swinging its heavy horns, something of a primeval, irresistible force. After a dramatic pause he would say to the newly arrived Columban, "Consider the *carabao;* study his ways; learn from him. He moves slowly, slowly, slowly. But he gets there just the same."

Patience will be tested in a thousand little ways as the missionary seeks to become "at home" in the land of his adoption. He needs a lot of the boll weevil in him, the one that was the subject of a song sung by the cotton pickers of the South. In the song they propose to place the boll weevil in the sand, in hot ashes, in the river, and in other unlikely places, but the boll weevil's refrain is always: "That'll be ma HOME! That'll be ma HOOME!"

No matter where the missionary goes he needs to feel at home. He ought not to feel like a visitor or a guest. He needs to steep himself in his parishioners' way of doing things and tamper with their traditions as little as possible.

This takes imagination, flexibility, adaptability, and patience. It doesn't mean giving up his principles or "going native." It means caring about the hopes and fears of the people and identifying with them, something as difficult to explain as it is to do.

A nun said, "We 'grow up' on the missions so that color, climate, food become so familiar we cease to notice them. We must be as interested as the people themselves in preserving the good customs of time immemorial, customs so dear to them.

When we really care about their culture they notice it and recognize us as friends."

There is a possibility that when a missionary has learned to love the traditions he will lose patience when he sees them vulgarized. For example, the All Souls gatherings in the cemeteries have been spoiled by loud transistor radios. Instead of singing carols at Christmas some people go from house to house and from *barrio* to *barrio* carrying a transistorized record player with a Beatles record or Bing Crosby dreaming of a white Christmas. They play the records at full volume only a few feet away until someone gives them a few *centavos* to go away.

A young missionary had to concentrate on the need for patience when he saw two men start to tear a hole in the wall of a newly completed church. They explained that it is unlucky to take twins out of the same door after baptism.

He also prayed for patience when a young couple were several hours late for their wedding. They arrived disheveled and muddy explaining that they had been trying to catch an escaped pig which was destined for the wedding breakfast.

A Columban said, "It is not easy when tired and hungry to go to work again when summoned. To have a busy *fiesta* morning in a village with confessions, marriages, sung Mass, procession. Then do thirty baptisms, pack the kit, mount the horse, hot and hungry. Then to be hailed by a latecomer to do baptism thirty-one. This is killing. It often happens."

Interruptions are a part of a missionary's vocation. During sleep, at meals, or even at prayer, interruptions punctuate the hours. As an example, a Columban recalled going into his tin-roofed church to pray. It was empty for the moment of worshipers, but no sooner had he taken out his rosary and completed the Creed than three little children came in just to watch him. "They were barefooted, raggedy, and just a little longer than an ear of corn." They kept their liquid brown eyes glued on him as they wiggled closer and closer to inspect the white soutane. As the little girl reached for the beads and toyed with the cross, one of the boys used his finger to explore the contour of Father's ear.

The priest was trying to focus on the mystery of the Annunciation when he felt a tap on the shoulder. It was Melinda, a high-school girl, whose friend had given her a scapular as a present and she wanted to be enrolled right now. After the brief ceremony the priest returned to his pew and marshalled all his thoughts on the Visitation.

Old José dropped in to have a chat with the Lord, and finding the pastor present included him in the conversation. José wanted to discuss last Sunday's sermon, especially the parts he felt had been omitted.

Just as José left, Isabel arrived with her sister, visiting from a neighboring village. Would Father tell her sister the history of the parish?

Pedro arrived during the Presentation in the Temple. He was in an expansive mood. He spoke of what wonderful weather it was for softball and said he was considering arranging a game with the Holy Name Society of a neighboring parish. By the way, would Father order some more Holy Name pins? And do come to the christening on Sunday.

During the Finding of the Child in the Temple, a delegation of school children hurriedly brought Father the latest news from the outside world. It seems all sorts of lawlessness had broken loose while he was at prayer. Some bold, bad boys had actually dared to climb the bell tower. Others, equally naughty, are at this minute pulling up the flowers in front of the church. The visitors make it clear that they would not dream of climbing bell towers or of pulling up flowers. They are so good that surely they have earned a rosary or a holy card. The pastor settles for holy cards; the children accept them with solemnity, plop in genuflections to all points of the compass, and clatter down the aisle into the brilliant sunshine.

The Columban was annoyed with himself for feeling annoyed. He had to keep reminding himself that it may have been the best rosary he said that year.

"If you adopt the culture of the Filipinos you can get anything you want," said Archbishop Cronin. "If you are dictatorial you get nothing. If you approach them in the right way they will give you things they shouldn't."

It is nice when a missionary comes to the Philippines knowing right off that he is in a Christian country and spared the oppressive weight of paganism that was felt by the Columbans in China. But this too, can be a disadvantage. It can fool the new missionary into forgetting that the Philippines are located in the East. The archbishop said that the Columbans in China and Korea never had to remind themselves that they were in the Orient, that was evident wherever the eye fell. In the Philippines, however, where the people speak English, wear western clothes, and adopt western fads, the tendency is to forget how Eastern they are.

Even the educated Filipino, with a Spanish name and speaking fluent English, often behaves differently from what might be expected of a westernized Asian. His value system is different from that current in the western world. The vast majority of forty million Filipinos demonstrate a mentality close to their Malayan forefathers. The Spanish influences, from 1521 to 1898, and the American, from 1898 to 1946, are not so deeply seated as one might expect.

In observing the value system, the first lesson to learn anywhere in the East is never to cause another *hiya,* or "loss of face." That is no light matter. Violence and tragedy often occur when face is lost. Sensitivity to *hiya* is needed in all matters large and small.

A missionary gave an example of how one needs imagination and patience to get small things done his way without causing hurt feelings. His cook thought that any water the least bit warm could be considered boiled. The priest, mistrusting the water, wanted to be sure it was seething thoroughly but didn't seem to be able to put across the idea. Finally he bought a kettle that whistles when a head of steam is built up, and so now the cook knows how to judge when the water is at the boil.

A pastor should understand, said Archbishop Cronin, that the need to save face causes some of his parishioners to fail in their religious duties. It is usual for someone to miss Mass on Sunday because of lacking new clothes, or to delay the baby's baptism indefinitely because there isn't enough money for a grand celebration.

The archbishop's former classmate, Father Chapman, said: "In dealing with people you must respect everyone. If you don't respect them in your heart they will know it. That means respecting the attractive and the unattractive, the good and the bad.

"You'll need patience because you are going to be wrong so often. Only through patience will you find out how wrong you are.

"The Filipinos are very sensitive to your reactions, especially to the reaction of anger. In their speech they are soft, and mild in manner, but if they do get angry there is no length to which they will not go. So anger terrifies them. They don't know that you can be angry without going too far. If they see that you will always be patient it gives them confidence in you."

The missionary needs also to have patience with the people he left behind. Frequently, the principles he teaches will be broken in a dramatic way back home. How can he effectively preach "by this men shall know that you are my disciples, if you love one another as I have loved you," when the evening news features stories of violence and injustice in Christian countries?

In speaking of this discrepancy, John Cardinal Wright said, "Perhaps the missioner of centuries past was a happier creature, in a way, than his counterpart today because, although it took him six months to a year to reach the land he was sent to evangelize, his hearers were educated only to the pure doctrine imparted by his catechesis, unpolluted by aberrant theories and examples from his homeland. Today's missioner, however, frequently has to endure more competition from his fellow Christians at home than he experiences from unbelieving rivals in the local mission field."

Patience comes easier, Archbishop Cronin believes, once you realize how much human nature is alike everywhere. Characteristics vary in intensity from person to person but every one carries within himself all the seeds of humanity. Even in the most noble of characters there are fenced off areas that hold out against God. And in the most disheveled characters there will be an oasis of sanctity. The archbishop believes that whatever faults you find in your parishioners you will find in the people back home. And find in yourself.

31 ✣ Patience
with the Situation

At a dinner for Columbans in Manila, Archbishop Cronin began his talk by humorously comparing pioneering days with the present: "When young missionaries arrive now, they know more theology than we did. They soon speak the language with more fluency. They are more sophisticated. Some of them even step from the airplane asking, "Who are the oppressed and where are the oppressors?"

He realizes that the situation that prevails could be better, and agrees with something the late President Magsaysay said: "I believe that the little man is fundamentally entitled to a little more food in his stomach, a little more clothing on his back, and a little more roof over his head."

The archbishop observed, "In the old days we went to the poor and said in effect, "We will baptize you and marry you and bury you, but if your roof leaks and your landlord is about to evict you, that is not our problem. Now we have more concern for justice in the world. At times we may become excessive in that concern, but it is one we must have."

To ignore the problems of justice, liberation, development, and peace, as Pope Paul said, "would be to forget the lesson that comes to us from the Gospel concerning love of our neighbor who is suffering and in want."

In his concern for justice the archbishop realizes that there are extremes that must be avoided. As the Asian bishops said in their report, they need to find ways to eradicate stark poverty without fostering the spirit of materialism, which is not a happy spirit.

Nor can the missionary allow himself to become no more than a social worker. A Columban said, "A missionary must give himself and his faith. Government social programs often turn sour because the bureaucratic system has no spiritual concerns. A social worker cares about material poverty; a missionary adds to that a concern for spiritual poverty. He is deeply aware of hungers other than those for bread. If he lacks that double concern, he might become an annoyance. It is hard to do things for people and not be hated for it. St. Vincent de Paul cautioned his followers to deport themselves so that the poor 'will forgive you the bread you gave them.' ''

The archbishop knows that missionaries must keep their sensitivity to human suffering, but not let that sensitivity paralyze them with despair or ineffective anger. He has come to see how the missionary struggles with a Christian paradox: realizing the value of pain and trying to relieve it. He is old enough to realize that no one can know the fulness of life without struggling toward it under the weight of the cross; as the great Quaker, William Penn, titled an essay, "No Cross, No Crown." And yet one of the missionary tasks is to help share, or relieve, the weight of the cross wherever he might find it.

During his forty years in the Philippines, Archbishop Cronin has done his utmost to relieve the pain and the agony which he shared with his people. He has lived with the heartache and the suffering caused by natural and man-made upheavals—earthquakes, tidal waves, hurricanes, floods, famine, the Japanese occupation, the Huk rebellion, the Muslim-Christian conflict, and martial law. He has seen changes come both slowly and with an unexpected swiftness. His experience has taught him to put his trust in God and to be patient.

The archbishop does not anticipate that the present situation will change overnight. He knows that really deep and lasting changes won't come next week, just because you want it so. As he said, "There won't be any changes until the people themselves become aware of the need for change to a better and more just world."

To help bring about these changes the missionary must work *with* the people, not just *for* the people. He must be sensitive to their values. He must respect their customs and culture, their way of doing things. It was with this in mind that Bishop Tudtud of Marawi, a diocese recently cut off from Archbishop's Cronin's archdiocese, advised missionaries who work with his countrymen: "Help us to discover our own riches; don't judge us poor because we lack what you have. Help us discover our chains; don't judge us slaves by the type of shackles you wear. Be patient with us as a people; don't judge us backward simply because we don't follow your stride. Be patient with our pace; don't judge us lazy simply because we can't follow your tempo. Be with us and proclaim the richness of your life which you can share with us. Be with us and be open to what we can give. Be with us as a companion who walks with us—neither behind nor in front—in our search for life and ultimately for God!"

Archbishop Cronin is the living embodiment of this advice. This is how he has lived and worked. As his fellow Columban, Bishop Henry Byrne of Iba, said, "Archbishop Cronin's greatest trait has been his love and respect for the Filipinos."

32 ✠ Patience with Yourself

A rchbishop Cronin feels that having patience with yourself is often more difficult than having patience with the people or with the situation that prevails. Such things as shyness, difficulty with the language, homesickness, and loneliness can drain a man's energy and lead him to the edge of despair.

A Columban who has always found shyness a problem said: "In the beginning you are almost sure to feel ill at ease at any gathering. You will lack poise and confidence when conversation is difficult. You'll seem aloof and uninterested in those you meet. You'll retire to a corner or focus on some one person. You'll nurse an overwhelming desire to escape. Be patient with yourself. Just remember you are not the first one this has happened to."

Slowness in learning a language can make a young missionary impatient with himself. The language school has eased this problem a great deal and yet it has brought a mixed blessing. One of the old hands said it can lead to a false sense of security: "When they come to learn the language everything bows to that. They learn it, most do anyway, well and quickly. But language is never the main thing. Kinship of spirit is more important than language. The important thing is that a man be patient and kind and have a sense of humor. The gift of laughter is a blessing—especially laughter directed at yourself. Teresa of Avila said, *'Lord preserve us from sour saints.'* "

Father Chapman, with forty years in the Philippines, has words of encouragement for the missionary who feels inadequate. He said that when a priest sees others more eloquent, more gifted with the language, more able to entertain, he ought not to be discouraged, but ought to say to himself: "I may not be particularly intelligent or at ease with administration, but this need not destroy my ministry. If I had these talents it would help, but I don't need them to do God's will. Had I needed them they would have been given to me. I have been sent to influence a certain group of people. In order to influence them I must be faithful to the instructions given by Christ. And that is all I have to do."

The old hands say that when a missionary feels lacking he should be aware that God puts you in impossible situations, and then if you trust him, he gives you improbable victories. Speaking to this point, a Columban sister observed, "If you knew in advance what you would be asked to do you would never come here. That's because you underrate yourself. When you find yourself in a situation that demands much of you, then quite suddenly you discover talents you never knew you had."

It is not unusual for a missionary to suffer homesickness, an uneasy, restless feeling of time passing slowly with a deep-down pang that won't go away. Of this, Father Frank McEnnis said, "Be aware that sooner or later you will feel the lure of the East. You look forward to going home, but after you are there a short time you will feel the East pulling at you."

Persistent loneliness might make a missionary lose patience with himself. The best defense against such loneliness, says Archbishop Cronin, is to keep occupied. As a spiritual director advised: "If you've no other work to do, break up the furniture and put it together again, rather than be idle."

Father McEnnis is thankful to an old priest who advised him that he could do worse than to take to Mindanao the Loeb edition of the classics. In time he either read all the things he had been told to read in school but hadn't, or he reread in depth books previously read.

"I had no radio or television," he said, "I would sit out there in the *barrio* reading some thick novel by Tolstoi or Dostoevski. Ah, it was wonderful! Then I'd go back home and get nothing read. Life there was too fragmented."

Missionaries today are more apt to be lonely than the pioneers, said Father Chapman. "We went through the depression years and so everybody's belt was tightened. When you don't have things you don't miss them. It is when you have things to lean on and then they are taken away from you that you miss them. In the seminary it was drummed into us every day, by men who had been on the missions, that we must be ready 'to take things hard.' So we were prepared for hardship.

"Another thing that helped us: we drew strength from the sacraments. Today we speak of liberating ourselves from the enemies without. It's the enemies within that are the great problem. We are liberated only when we master our own inner selves."

Patience has a place in spiritual development, too. In the seminary Father Harris used to tell the Columbans that there is no instant holiness; spiritual maturity usually comes more gradually than physical maturity. He said that sanctity is not something arrived at, but a way of traveling. The priesthood, too, is a pilgrimage. Father Harris considered life as something of a prolonged spiritual retreat in which you meet two strangers, yourself and God.

A Columban said that Archbishop Goodier had some consoling thoughts for people, such as missionaries, who often find themselves in what seem impossible situations. In speaking of the wisdom of putting things in God's hands, Goodier said: "Nothing in the hands of God is evil. Not failure, not frustration of every hope or ambition, not death itself. All in his hands is success. All will bear fruit the more we leave it to him, having no ambitions, no preoccupations, no excessive preferences or desires of our own."

33 ✛ The Council and After

Patrick Cronin, like other missionaries, felt encouraged when Angelo Roncalli, of the village of Sotto il Monte, was elected to the papacy in 1958. He felt sure that here was a man exceptionally aware of the missions. Especially when the new pope made it immediately clear that as John XXIII he would be a pastoral pope, one who would devote himself to spreading the word of God and the Church in the world.

Angelo Roncalli was well known for his interest in evangelization. At age forty he had been summoned to Rome by Pope Benedict XV, and there, in 1921, took over the Society for the Propagation of Faith, an organization interested in the development of foreign missions. He was so successful in increasing assistance to missionary effort that in 1925 he was created an archbishop.

When Pope John decided that it was time for another Vatican Council, Patrick Cronin left Mindanao, in October of 1962, to attend the opening of it. He arrived in Rome feeling optimistic, for by now he realized that every age calls for a new response from the Church.

After having attended all four sessions of the council, he finds himself in almost a hundred percent agreement with what was done there. He feels there should be a council every fifty years, perhaps more often. Councils should not come too close together, though, because it takes time to absorb all the conclusions from one. "We still haven't absorbed all the conclusions from the last one."

Patrick Cronin observes that: "The council brought the Church into contact with the actual world. Its ecumenical spirit helped us realize that while the Christian world is twenty percent, still there is a non-Christian world of eighty percent.

Of course there were problems. Father William Brunner speaks lightly of some that were not amusing at the time. He begins his story with the hint of a sigh, "It's a long, long way from Rome to Kolambugan."

His trouble began on December 4, 1963, when the fathers of the Second Vatican Council published the Constitution on the Sacred Liturgy. The document took several months to reach Kolambugan and was received with a mixture of enthusiasm and dismay, mostly the latter.

The church rests near the summit of a deeply wooded hill looking down on the town and out across the blue water of Panquil Bay to tall mountains behind Ozamis City. From outside the church the view was majestic, but on the inside—oh, my! Statues, relics, and candles everywhere. Our Lady in a variety of poses. Our Lord decked out in purples, reds, and whites, with dust collecting in the folds. Everywhere candles gently drooped in the heat. Father Brunner said, "It was just the kind of place the council fathers had in mind when they said, 'Renew your churches!' "

Father Brunner and the pastor, Father William Smith, knew instinctively that renovations in Mindanao would involve problems that the council fathers had not foreseen. Even the Columbans in their most cautious conversations did not foresee some that eventually loomed along the way.

"The basic problem," explained Father Brunner, "is that Kolambugan has not quite made it into the machine age. Here everything is done by hand. Our wood is hand-sawed, hand-planed and hand-finished. Our walls are hand-scraped and hand-painted. Our concrete is hand-mixed.

"Not that we are fanatics for hand work, we just lack machines. Even when there are machines, they work erratically. Other people can send a space craft around the globe in ninety minutes, but down here among the palm trees it's not that way. We feel good when the two o'clock launch arrives by three, even when there is no breakdown."

When the renovation began, water was the first problem. Hundreds of gallons would be needed to cement and plaster. But water is scarce, even the undrinkable kind. It's still hawked around town in carts, or by a yoke draped over the shoulder with little pails attached to each end. Some Columbans in a neighboring parish loaned a two-wheel water wagon; someone else loaned a gas-operated cement mixer.

"Getting materials up the hill was an interesting venture" said Father Brunner "especially during torrential rains. The roads! Transporting fragile items requires some caution and much prayer."

Money, of course, was another problem. But the people wanted a renewed church, of that they were sure. With enthusiasm, a committee agreed to run *fiestas* and dances and other activities to raise funds. Little by little they paid for salaries, sand, gravel, steel.

Several breakdowns at the cement factory slowed the project. So did soaring prices and unending discussions—to give the details would be too painful. Somehow or other the church was finally complete, about four years from the day the council fathers had published their document in Rome.

From the entrance the wide aisle leads to the simple white Altar of Sacrifice. Behind the main altar is a massive cross adorning the back wall. On either side of the altar are the lecterns for the commentator and celebrant. To the left of the sanctuary is the choir, in an alcove that once housed burning candles. Sections of the communion rail have been removed so that the people can receive the sacrament standing.

"The dedication ceremonies took place early in 1968," said Father Brunner. "Crepe-paper streamers flew from the trees. Flowering palms in tall urns decorated the entrance. It was a joyous day, all right."

One of the things that has pleased the archbishop most about Vatican II is that it brought a greater awareness of lay people's responsibility in the Church. A good lay person used to be one who went to Mass on Sunday, received the sacraments, and said daily prayers. Now the movement is toward more participation with the priest in all the affairs of the Church.

This new awareness of the role of the laity in the Church is seen by Archbishop Cronin as "the key to restoring the faith to the Philippines." In 1973 he began a program to train lay leaders. Eight or ten men and women are chosen from each village and given a course of training at a diocesan center. The groups learn how to conduct a Sunday liturgy in the village chapel when the priest can't be present. They are trained to prepare children and adults for confession, communion, and confirmation, and to instruct couples for marriage. In general, they learn to perform the many services people need to help them lead full Catholic lives in the family and in the community. "The zeal of our first trainees and the response of the people," said the archbishop, "have been wonderful."

The trauma of Vatican II, and it was that, has also left some uneasiness. But all in all, the archbishop finds the Church more free, more healthy and more pleasant than it was a generation ago. Certainly it is more humble.

While changes were being encouraged by Vatican II, a growing national consciousness brought other changes into the lives of missionaries.

The archbishop said, "The red carpet is less red now. People are touchy. A bishop is looking for priests who understand this. They must cherish the culture of the country. They need to learn from the people. Gandhi said, 'There go my people. I must follow them because I am their leader.' "

The archbishop wants so much to identify with his people that he became a citizen of the Philippines in 1969. This allows him to vote and to take part in community life in a way an outsider cannot.

In speaking of new attitudes toward missionary work, Father P. J. McGlinchey, a Columban, said, "There are those who say that the westerner should leave the people of the so-called underdeveloped countries alone. They point out that the westerner, by bringing in foreign ideas and methods, only serves to disrupt the even pattern of life by creating all kinds of problems which did not previously exist. He also creates needs. He inevitably brings in some of the worst features of western life."

Father McGlinchey, who has spent twenty-five years in Korea, came to Manila in August of 1975 to receive the Ramon Magsaysay Award for International Understanding. The award of $10,000, the most prestigious in Asia, recognizes persons in Asia who show concern for the have-nots of the world.

After receiving the honor, Father McGlinchey discussed in the Columbans' magazine, *Columban Mission,* whether or not western missionaries should leave the underdeveloped countries alone. "There is something to be said for this argument when it is applied to certain aspects of Asian life which are in fact superior to life in the west. However, in the opinion of this writer, the blanket statement that nothing should be done to change the pattern of life in the undeveloped areas, is unacceptable for the simple reason that there are many aspects of life in these areas which urgently demand change for the better."

Father McGlinchey feels that the western temperament is often impatient with the status quo and that a more circumspect approach could be more effective. The westerner feels compelled to rush forward along a straight line trying to reach his object today, while experience has shown that a more subtle approach achieves more in the long run.

"The peasant has very little material goods," writes Father McGlinchey, "but one thing he clings to is his pride. He does not want to be beholden to anybody, especially to a foreigner. If, therefore, the foreigner wishes to help this man by implanting new ideas and introducing new methods, he must take great care to create the impression at least that these ideas are springing not from himself but from the mind of the local peasant. This can be done in a variety of ways. But the first requirement always is that the foreigner must present a low profile in both word and action. This is much easier said than done."

Archbishop Cronin was pleased with the Apostolic Exhortation, *Evangelization,* that Pope Paul issued at the end of 1975. In the document the Pope rejected the idea sometimes proposed in the West that teaching religion to either children or adults is a violation of religious liberty. The Pope said it would be wrong to impose something on the consciences of others, but to propose to their consciences the message of the Gospel is no attack on religious liberty.

The Pope rejected the views of those who would confine the work of the Church entirely to social betterment. He granted that working for a better life on earth is a worthwhile objective, but the Church cannot confine its labor to the solution of temporal problems.

He also rejected the idea that violence, especially force of arms, is necessary for human liberation and freedom: "We exhort you not to place your trust in violence and revolution. That is contrary to the Christian spirit, and it can also delay instead of advance that social uplifting to which you lawfully aspire. We must say and reaffirm that violence is not in accord with the Gospel and that it is not Christian."

Archbishop Cronin is pleased that the Second Vatican Council, the Synod of Bishops in Rome, and the Asian Catholic Conference all insisted on evangelization as the highest priority of the Church. The Asian Catholic Conference summed it up in a sentence: "The mission of the Church is primarily to lead men to repentance, and to a turning of the heart to Jesus as Lord."

Vatican II and nationalism are making missionaries more aware than ever that they are to develop a local clergy and move on— in other words, to work themselves out of a job. Or as Patrick Cronin put it, "The highest aim of the missionary is to make himself superfluous."

The archbishop quotes some statistics with a certain amount of pride: of the sixteen bishops on Mindanao, twelve are Filipino. Of the 700 priests at least half are Filipino. His old diocese of Ozamis is now divided into three—Ozamis, Iligan, and Marawi—with a Filipino bishop in each. In Pagadian, in the province of Zamboanga, where Patrick Cronin worked as a pastor, a Filipino bishop is in charge. The Auxiliary Bishop of Cagayan de Oro, Bishop Ireneo Amantillo, is a Filipino Redemptorist.

As a droll Columban observed, "Our aim is to entrust one diocese after another to local clergy and retire. We're waiting for the last sacraments and a happy death."

34 ✛ A Walk in the Evening

Archbishop Cronin tells his young priests, "Say your prayers and take a stroll every evening." He finds both activities forms of communication. During prayer one communes with God, and during the stroll with God's creation.

The need for prayer is one thing about missionary work that has not changed, of that the archbishop feels sure. He believes in St. Augustine's observation that he who prays well lives well, and he knows what Pope Paul meant when he said that without prayer a Christian's life is like a blown-out candle.

Missionary service, if it is not to pall, springs from a sense of divine vocation sustained by a supernatural motive and supported by an interior life of prayer. Since everything a priest does needs to be done in the light of the priesthood, with nothing compartmentalized, prayer must touch every aspect of his life. It is prayer that brings the grace to appraise the things of time in the light of eternity.

Grace, that's the thing. Patrick Cronin is acutely aware of the truth of something a Columban wrote a decade ago: Father John O'Hehir received a letter from halfway across the world saying, "Let me know what you need urgently, Father, and I will try and send it to you." The missionary thought most carefully before answering this wonderfully generous person. He said, "I could have immediately sent a list longer than any ever taken to the supermarket. But the word 'urgent' made me hesitate, and ask for but one thing—more Grace. Yes, more Grace. Our primary mission need is Grace."

The archbishop is impressed by how God can break into life in new and startling ways. Now that he is old enough he realizes that God is the author of the unexpected and that his ways of running the world are more interesting than ours. Instead of telling the Almighty what ought to happen it is better to listen more; it is the listening that brings alertness to stirrings of the Holy Spirit within.

The archbishop admits that conditions for such listening seemed more favorable forty years ago. The hours spent walking through the close, endless monotony of forest sapped energy of body and mind, but there was time for prayer. Riding a horse over miles of empty trails had advantages, too, for then a priest could enter into silence, stilling activities of mind, allowing intuitions and feelings to rise from the depths.

Now Archbishop Cronin lurches across bad roads surrounded by noisy, defective motors, honking horns, and choking dust. Drivers hurtle through space; to go more slowly would mean a loss of face. The archbishop and his driver recite the rosary and a litany:

Hail Mary (HONK! HONK!) full of grace (HONK!) hallowed be thy name (HONK! HONK! HONK!) . . . Tower of Ivory (VAROOM!) Morning Star (VAROOM! VAROOM!)

Yet amid the commotion they are surrounded by saints. They pass the San Pedro rice mill, the Lourdes beauty parlor, and the Immaculate Conception pharmacy. Hundreds of poorly clad children swarm to the road from the *barrios* bearing such names as Noberto, Mateo, Marciano, Francisca, and Apollonia. A bus from the San Antonio Service Line narrowly escapes colliding with a truck displaying across its hood the supplication, "Holy Mary Pray for Me," and well she might.

The days of such adventurous travel are not entirely behind Patrick Cronin, even though he does spend much time at a desk. A few years ago, when he was still a bishop, he and Father Paul O'Rourke went on a hectic five-day journey to confirm about 2,000 Filipinos. The trip was such that Father O'Rourke wrote a magazine piece about it. One incident will suffice to give the flavor:

When the outboard rigger was ready to take the priest, the bishop, and a houseboy on the first leg of the journey, not one of the local fishermen had ventured out, for the sea was too rough. The boatman assured the bishop that by hugging the coast he could make it safely, but after an hour's ride the light craft was forced out to sea to avoid sharp pieces of coral that threatened to rip the bottom to shreds. When the waves were at their highest the engine gave a few coughs and died.

"Don't panic," the boatman said. He had his screwdriver and

all would be fixed in a jiffy. The jiffy turned out to be more than an hour. The boat was being tossed at the mercy of the waves, and with not another vessel in sight. The small craft was carried far out to sea. The boatman himself began to panic.

"Then we spotted a big diesel inboard boat," said Father O'Rourke. "The bishop and I stood up and began to wave our hands. The sea was too rough for this. We almost got tossed overboard. So I stood up and the bishop and the houseboy held me while I waved frantically. The long white cassock finally caught the eyes of their helmsman. They began to head in our direction. It took them about twenty minutes to reach us and then the real fun began. They couldn't get a line on us because of the heavy seas. After about five minutes one of their crew members dived in with the two ropes and finally made us secure."

It took the big boat about an hour to get in close enough to shore to transfer its passengers to a smaller boat. This one got them in still closer. Finally the bishop, priest, and houseboy took off their socks and shoes and waded to the beach.

A sense of adventure, an inner push toward it, is almost essential to a missionary. To this should be added the kind of toughness of body and spirit that Patrick Cronin brought with him. This forms the basis for the courage a missionary needs to endure the suffering, the dominant motif of his world. Illness, loneliness, weariness—the various faces of suffering—are as much a part of his life as eating and sleeping.

While the dramatic adventure of the open sea, mountain path, and jungle trail is less a part of his life now, the archbishop's day is still far from mundane. It begins in darkness. As a Columban said, "The cocks start to crow when the dogs stop barking." At four o'clock the curfew ends and immediately all the combustion engines of buses, cars, jeeps, and motorcycles rev up. What a cacophony from all those faulty engines and defective mufflers! Add to this transistor radios turned up full volume and tuned to local stations that specialize in the most blatant acid rock. The church doesn't help any with its tradition of ringing bells for half an hour before Mass. The bell begins with the clanging of a fire brigade, settles down to a more gentle tolling, and returns to clanging a few minutes before the start of Mass.

It is still fairly cool when the archbishop arises in the *convento,* a two-story cement house built in the Spanish manner with high ceilings, wood and tile floors, cross ventilation, and wide verandahs. From the back verandah is a view of a lazy curve in the Cagayan River, with coconut palms, banana plantations, and dense tangle growing to the water's edge. From dawn until nightfall families come gliding down hidden paths, enter the shallow stream to bathe and wash clothes. A backdrop to all of this heavy greenery is the misty outline of the Bukidnon mountains, softened by a tinge of mauve.

The scene from the back verandah is that of the old Philippines; from the front, it is of the new. There is a circular park, a quarter mile in diameter, featuring a fountain spurting a twenty-foot stream. At dawn the park is alive with adults performing calisthenics and children playing games, for there is still a thin coolness that allows for activity, like a thin coating over a heaviness that warns of things to come.

In a few steps, the archbishop reaches the cathedral, a fairly modern building. The old one was bombed out of existence because the Japanese reasoned that since Americans do not bomb churches why not store ammunition in the *convento* and in the cathedral. When Fertig learned of this he passed the word along to MacArthur's headquarters.

So, one September day in 1944, the Americans sent eighty-two planes to hit Cagayan harbor, and, in passing, dropped a few bombs on the *convento* and cathedral. A series of explosions rocked the town. An old Filipino decided this was the start of The Aid he had been praying for for three years. Observing the nearness of Japanese soldiers, he whispered to his nephews, "Keep happy in your hearts, but look sad and sympathetic in your faces."

When the archbishop returns from Mass, beggars are waiting at the door of the *convento.* He listens to each and either gives a few coins or sends them to the House of Friendship which he established in Cagayan. There a nun provides them with shelter —a bed in a screened room—and helps them get back to their homes.

The archbishop settles at his desk hoping to get some paper work finished before a parade of petitioners begins to move through his office. Beneath the glass on the desk top is a street map of Cagayan de Oro with parish boundaries outlined, and pictures of a Madonna, St. Joseph, and the Sacred Heart. On top of the desk stand a metal crucifix and a small flag of the Philippines. Behind the archbishop's head hang a photograph of Pope John and a map of the Islands.

The first petitioner of the morning might be a young priest who wants to do away with the parish structure and try something different. Or a nun who needs more money to finance her projects. Next might come a young couple who want to get married immediately even though they lack the proper papers; they explain that they can't wait because the wedding invitations have been printed. And then there are those who come to chat. In every case the archbishop makes the visitor feel welcome, no matter how frayed his nerve ends might be as the day's heat increases. And so the hours pass with the coming and going of people who bring with them more problems than solutions.

Darkness descends suddenly in the tropics. It often finds the archbishop and his visitors sitting in bamboo and rattan chairs on the upstairs verandah looking toward the river and having a sip of rum before supper. Lizards dart up the walls and across the ceiling, making a clicking sound in pursuit of each other, a sound that might mean anger or affection, it is hard to tell.

The lizards remind the archbishop of the old days in Molave. It was known for its wild life—mosquitos, black ants, gnats, leeches, snakes, and scorpions. Snakes often were found in beds. Scorpions hid beneath the lip of plates, and so it was best to run a knife blade under each before lifting it.

When the group moves from the dark verandah to the yellow light in the dining room there are almost sure to be several guests at the table. The archbishop once confided to a friend, "People say, 'You have a big house here.' As though that is a great luxury. It would be a great luxury to have a small house. If a bishop wanted to be selfish he would live in a humble house with his office at some distance away and he would keep office hours, as most professional men do. When you have a big house—certainly on the missions—it is filled with visitors most of the time. You get no privacy. No rest. It's best, though, to keep a big house open to all of the priests. They need a place to come to."

At the dinner table a young Filipino priest has just come in from some remote part of the diocese, thin and worn. The archbishop asks, "You need any money?" He looks shy and says, no. Little by little everyone at the table tells his troubles: Someone is trying to poison the well in the *barrio* . . . a plague of locusts is destroying the crops . . . an ex-nun has been arrested on charges of radical activity.

Some of the anecdotes are on the lighter side: A missionary wondered why the big holy water font at the back of his church was empty each evening, even though he filled it at noon. He found the answer when he caught a parishioner's horse drinking from it.

This animal anecdote reminds one of the archbishop's visitors to tell of his experiences with rats. Most nights he is awakened by something brushing against his hand or cheek. In the dim glow of a flashlight there is a scurry throughout the room. He has taken to shooting his guests with an air rifle.

Someone else says that rats destroy one-third of the rice crop. Since the Philippines needs to import only ten percent of its rice for consumption, if the rats were gone the Islands could actually export some rice.

A more statistical minded visitor recalls that he read somewhere that rats outnumber people twelve to one in the Philippines. A female gives birth to from six to sixteen in a litter and this is repeated six to ten times a year. If left undisturbed a pair would have 330,000 offspring in three years.

After the evening meal the archbishop goes for a stroll. Dressed in a white soutane, with red buttons, he walks, with hands clasped behind back, around the circular park. He puts aside what he has heard that day about ambushes, typhoons, and earthquakes to give attention to the overhanging filagree of the mimosa trees, the fragrance of blossoms, and the night breeze in the palms.

Young couples come out from behind the *convento,* because after dark a guard clears them from the grassy plot above the river, ending their "pre-Cana conference," as the archbishop puts it. Children, as they pass on their evening *pasao* ("stroll") sing out "Good evening Monsignor." (In the Philippines bishops and archbishops are addressed as monsignor.) Some children press the back of his hand to their foreheads, an old custom, called the *besa*. He pauses to talk with adults sitting around the fountain. Like many Occidentals who speak to Filipinos a great deal, he has the habit of putting "huh?" at the end of sentences, a way of saying, "Do you understand?" If someone speaks of future plans the archbishop says, "Please God," stressing the last word in a way that indicates, "If it pleases God."

Walking around the park he wonders about the future. He fears the bishops of the Far East were right when they agreed that "The trend in most of the Asian countries points in the direction of a serious curtailment of religious freedom." They believe that ministers of the Church, like the first Christians, will have to find ways and means of spreading the Gospel under trying conditions, and that anyone training for the ministry in the Far East needs to be prepared for ever increasing difficulties.

Archbishop Cronin does not feel that this testing of religion in Asia means a lessening of evangelization. A missionary must continue to be present to bring about occasions at which an individual may respond to grace. As Cardinal Suenens wrote: "Go, said Jesus, announce the Gospel. He did not say that men would accept it. He simply said that it must be announced to them, presented to them, that they might be tempted to believe in it."

The missionary in the Far East will continue to help his parishioners, not merely to survive but to live lives that might worthily be called human. In bringing this about he needs to be careful not to give the impression that a new materialistic philosophy is needed and that secularization makes men free.

The word free is much used in Asia these days in every facet of life—political, social, economic, religious. Will the common man be equal to the adventure of such freedom? In trying to answer, the archbishop is hesitant, realizing that there is always an element of surprise in the unfolding of great changes. The expression, "Who would have thought it!" has been echoing down the ages.

During the evening stroll the past, too, is part of Patrick Cronin's thoughts and conversations. He finds himself recalling, more and more, the years of development, from 1952 until 1970, when his energy was at its peak and everything seemed to be happening at once in Ozamis. He built twenty-eight churches, a cathedral, a seminary, and a bishop's house; established fourteen new parishes, and opened twelve new schools. The development of the sacramental life can be suggested with one statistic: he confirmed 200,000 children.

As for thoughts of the present they are burdened with the sheer weight of numbers. For example when the Spanish gave the Philippines to the United States eighty years ago there were only eight million Filipinos. When Patrick Cronin arrived forty years ago there were sixteen million. Now there are forty million.

The proportion of priests to people in the archbishop's native Ireland is one to every 564 Catholics; in the Philippines it is one for every 5,638. In the Archdiocese of Cagayan de Oro there are half a million Catholics with only 61 priests, 110 sisters, and 3 brothers to care for them. Without the help of lay people the archbishop would feel more inundated than he does.

All of these statistics, trends, and problems keep him wondering why a boy from Moneygall and Tullamore should have all of this happening to him. He keeps trying to justify to himself his position in life. He knows how Major General William Sharp felt when in the dark days of Mindanao he said to a priest, "Padre, I have the stars of a general, but I wish I were only a colonel." While carrying the burdens of an archbishop, Patrick Cronin knows he would feel more at ease as a parish priest.

Someone said of Brother Lawrence, the seventeenth-century mystic, "All his life he took pains not to come into the stare of men." Something like this could be said of Patrick Cronin. Coming "into the stare of men" by being the subject of this biography has been a painful experience, one that he consented to endure only because his superior general had asked him.

When Father Richard Steinhilber was superior general of the Columbans, he said: "Archbishop Cronin tends to belittle himself. He wonders why he was made archbishop while there are so many other men more intelligent and more able. He makes a strong case against himself. You would be inclined to go along with it, except that all of a sudden you realize he is a man of strong intellectual interests. And he has a sort of country shrewdness that might be called wisdom."

Father James Corrigan, who came with Patrick Cronin as one of the Columban pioneers on Mindanao, wrote in a magazine article in December of 1963: "In every story of missionary enterprises, there are individuals and groups deserving a special word of commendation. First of all there is our own Bishop Cronin. His choice as Bishop of Ozamis was a happy one for us, for no one knew the diocese and its problems better than he, and over the past ten years since his appointment as chief pastor, he has displayed the keenest interest in every department of pastoral work. In his dealings with priests and people, he has always shown kindness and simplicity. When the people of his diocese meet him, they can feel the warmth and sincerity of this greeting. His zeal for the spiritual advancement of the people of his diocese is an inspiration to priests and people."

How fast the forty years have gone! The archbishop well remembers that early Sunday morning, December 11, 1938, when from the deck of the inter-island boat, the *Panay,* he had his first look at Mindanao. Bishop Hayes was standing beside him. The bishop had come up from Cagayan to Cebu to welcome the young priests. He had explained to them that he would transfer the province gradually from the administration of the Jesuits to the Columbans so that the transition would be easy for all concerned.

Bishop Hayes was full of vitality and plans that day. Patrick Cronin remembers this when he goes to visit the retired prelate, nearing ninety, in his small room in Maria Reyna Hospital in Cagayan de Oro. A Columban who accompanied Archbishop Cronin on one such visit said, "Here you have a preview of how you are going to spend your last days."

Patrick Cronin knows how he would like to spend his last days. Since he believes a bishop's concern should be mainly pastoral rather than administrative, an ideal difficult to live by, he would like to be a pastor once more. Say, in a parish of four or five thousand, a small one in the Philippines. This would give a sense of completing the cycle, of returning to beginnings. Such a rounding off could bring great satisfaction. But he will stay in his present post "long enough to let the young bishop get seniority," meaning the Most Rev. Ireneo Amantillo, D.D.

The archbishop finds satisfaction now in sticking it out. He has endured. It still surprises him. He hopes the old Columban was right who said, "In heaven I don't expect credit for coming on the missions. Ah, no. But I hope I get credit for staying."